Family Circle

BIG BOOK OF
CHRISTMAS

GREAT
HOLIDAY
RECIPES,
GIFTS AND
DECORATING
IDEAS

A LEISURE ARTS PUBLICATION

FamilyCircle

BIG BOOK OF
christmas

LEISURE ARTS
Vice President and Editor-in-Chief: Sandra Graham Case
Executive Director of Publications: Cheryl Nodine Gunnells
Publications Director: Susan White Sullivan
Editorial Director: Susan Frantz Wiles
Design Director: Cyndi Hansen
Photography Director: Lori Ringwood Dimond
Art Operations Director: Jeff Curtis

FAMILY CIRCLE
Editor-in-Chief: Susan Kelliher Ungaro
Executive Editor: Barbara Winkler
Food Director: Peggy Katalinich
How-To Editor: Peggy Greig

G+J USA PUBLISHING
Senior Vice President of New Business
    Development and Licensing: Daniel Rubin
Books & Licensing Manager: Lisa Kolodny

LEISURE ARTS EDITORIAL STAFF

EDITORIAL
Managing Editor: Alan Caudle
Associate Editor: Kimberly L. Ross

TECHNICAL
Managing Editor: Mary S. Hutcheson
Senior Editor: Sherry T. O'Connor
Copy Editors: Linda L. Garner, Valesha M. Kirksey
    and Lois J. Long
Production Assistant: Carol McElroy

FOODS
Foods Editor: Celia Fahr Harkey, R.D.
Copy Editor: Judy Millard

DESIGN
Design Manager: Diana Sanders Cates
Designers: Linda Diehl Tiano and Claudia Wendt
Craft Assistant: Lucy Beaudry

ART
Art Director: Mark Hawkins
Senior Production Artist: Mark R. Potter
Production Artists: Dana Vaughn and Matt Davis
Staff Photographer: Russell Ganser
Photography Stylists: Janna Laughlin and Cassie Newsome
Publishing Systems Administrator: Becky Riddle
Publishing Systems Assistants: Myra S. Means and
    Chris Wertenberger

PROMOTIONS
Associate Editor: Steven M. Cooper
Designer: Dale Rowett
Graphic Artist: Deborah Kelly

LEISURE ARTS BUSINESS STAFF

Publisher: Rick Barton
Vice President, Finance: Tom Siebenmorgen
Director of Corporate Planning and Development:
    Laticia Mull Cornett
Vice President, Retail Marketing: Bob Humphrey
Vice President, Sales: Ray Shelgosh

Vice President, National Accounts: Pam Stebbins
Director of Sales and Services: Margaret Reinold
Vice President, Operations: Jim Dittrich
Comptroller, Operations: Rob Thieme
Retail Customer Service Managers: Sharon Hall and Stan Raynor
Print Production Manager: Fred F. Pruss

Library of Congress Catalog Number 98-66514
Hardcover ISBN 1-57486-270-7
Softcover ISBN 1-57486-271-5

10 9 8 7 6 5 4 3 2

'Tis the Season

There are so many reasons to love Christmas — driving through neighborhoods awash with twinkling lights, festooning the tree with ornaments crafted by my children's hands, singing carols without worrying about being on key. But one of my most favorite things is working on projects with my daughter Christina. Recently I taught her to knit, as my mother showed me so many years ago. Now that she has the hang of it, Christina is working up a simple scarf that I know will be treasured by its recipient. To me, that type of exchange, sharing time and talent, gets to the heart of the holidays.

This book is brimming with ideas and how-to's perfectly in keeping with the spirit of give-and-take. Knit a nifty scarf, hat or purse. Stitch a special tree skirt that's sure to be passed along from generation to generation. Make an adorable Advent tree you can use to count down to the 25th year after year. All the instructions you need are right here.

As for incredible edibles, this book also offers recipes to round out your holiday repertoire. One suggestion I especially like is to host a breakfast party. The morning hours might not be ones you'd usually think of for a get-together, but check out the scrumptious possibilities: pecan-studded sticky buns, lemony muffins, decadent cappuccino-soaked French toast. I can't think of a better way to start a day than with a delicious breakfast in the company of friends. In addition, we offer plenty of other culinary inspiration, in the form of candies, cookies and much more.

Whether your creativity leads you and yours to the sewing machine or glue gun, mixer or stove, the result is sure to be the unique pride that results when someone admires a job done well, and with love.

Susan Ungaro

Susan Ungaro
Editor-in-Chief, Family Circle

contents

Peace, JOY, Love

TRIMMINGS TO LIFT THE SPIRIT

there's nothing more comforting than going **home** for the holidays. Casual *elegance* inspires family and friends to relax; a traditional color scheme bids "Welcome"; and the **spirit** of the season nestles close to our **hearts**.

How-To's on page 116

Festoon your tree with symbols of goodwill and holiday cheer. Letters painted cranberry-red and gold spell out the words Peace, Love and Joy. Pretty paper doves top the tree and hang from perches all over. Tiny French horns and trumpets complement sheet-music ornaments, while golden pears are eye-catching alternatives to colored balls.

How-To's on page 117

Turn the fireplace into an invitation to celebrate by layering baubles over an evergreen garland. Sew stockings to suit the tastes of everyone in the family. Cover a velvet tree skirt (opposite, top) with hints of holly. Thick gold bullion fringe is just the choice for a glorious finish. Glistening tassel ornaments (right) are fashioned from unfinished wooden finials.

8

VELVET TREE SKIRT

You need: $1^1/_2$ yds of 45"W rayon/acetate velvet; $1^1/_2$ yds of lining fabric; sewing supplies; spray water bottle with water; large holly rubber stamp; iron; paintbrush; gold metallic acrylic paint; 4 yds of gold bullion fringe; glue gun.

Cutting velvet and lining fabric: Cut a 44"-dia circle from velvet. Find the center and, on wrong side, mark a 6"-dia circle. Cut a straight slit from edge of skirt to outer edge of inner circle; cut out inner circle. Cut lining in same manner as velvet.

Embossing velvet: Lightly mist wrong side of velvet in area where stamp will be placed. Place stamp, image-side up, on ironing board. Lay velvet, right side down, on stamp. Using a dry iron set on wool or cotton, press fabric, without moving iron, for 20 seconds (use section of iron without holes). Lift iron. Repeat for each motif.

Adding lining: Pin skirt and lining together, right sides facing; stitch in $1/_4$" seam, leaving opening in slit for turning. Turn right side out; slipstitch opening closed.

Embellishing: Accent leaves and berries with gold paint. Glue fringe around outer edge of skirt.

TASSEL ORNAMENTS

You need: *Finial tops* – Assorted unfinished wooden parts (such as $1^1/_2$" round or oval knobs, wheels, candle cups, spools); wood glue; drill with $3/_{16}$" bit; paintbrushes; gesso; acrylic paints; antiquing medium; rag.

Tassels – Cardboard; assorted threads, thin yarns and ribbon (such as pearl cotton, nubby cotton yarn, $1/_8$" and $1/_{16}$" ribbons, thin metallic cord/thread, other textured threads); thin wire (for inserting tassel into finial); craft or fabric glue; scissors.

Making finial top: Experiment with different arrangements to make a multipiece finial, as long as bottom part is wide enough to accommodate finished tassel. Glue pieces together; dry completely. Drill a hole completely through assembly (from top down).

Continued on page 10

Painting: Prime finial with gesso; let dry. Paint as desired with acrylics. When dry, apply antiquing medium; wipe off excess with rag.

Making tassel: Cut two 3"W x 5"L pieces of cardboard. Hold pieces together and wrap thread around long side of cardboard, mixing colors and textures. Be sure all loose ends of threads end up on the same end of cardboard. When wrapping is completed, cut a short piece of any thread and slip it between cardboard pieces and wrapped threads on one end; knot securely. At the other end, insert blade of scissors and cut across threads. Remove cardboard. Tie a piece of thread around middle of bundle to secure threads temporarily.

Making twisted hanger: Cut a piece of thread four times longer than desired hanger length (hanger must go through all finial pieces); knot ends together. Hold knotted end and secure opposite ends on a doorknob. Pulling thread taut, twist thread in one direction until it begins to kink up on itself. Still keeping thread taut, fold the twisted thread in half so that knotted end meets secured end. Release tension so that thread twists together into a double twisted cord. Knot knotted end and secured end together and remove from doorknob. Slip twisted cord through top of tassel bundle; knot ends. Hide knot inside bundle.

Finishing: Cut a piece of wire (length depends on size of finial top) and bend wire into a U-shaped threader. Slip threader through hanger and push ends of wire up through hole in bottom of finial, forcing the bundle up into the hole. When you are sure bundle will fit properly, pull bundle down; apply some glue inside finial. Pull on threader again to reinsert bundle, pulling threader and hanger out through top of finial. Remove threader. Remove thread securing bundle; trim ends of finished tassel evenly; fluff out. If desired, glue threads or ribbons around finial top.

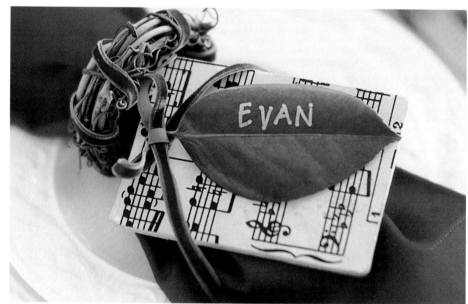

For a rich, but understated, table, choose natural neutrals. Mix up candlesticks to prevent the atmosphere from being too formal, and alternate variously tinted goblets. Guide guests to their seats with personalized napkin rings (above). To make them, weave velvet ribbon around a ready-made grapevine ring. Then write each person's name on a real leaf with a gold paint pen and add a sheet-music ornament. Tiny drawstring bags made from fancy fabric scraps are perfect for tying up tiny favors (top). Mix up colors and sizes for fun.

counting
the days

5 CLEVER WAYS
TO COUNT DOWN
THE SEASON

MAKE THE DAYS BEFORE CHRISTMAS A TREAT IN THEMSELVES! HANG SWEET

LITTLE GINGER PEOPLE ON AN ADVENT CALENDAR CHAIR. HIDE TINY TRINKETS

IN FELT ENVELOPES OR GOODY BAGS. DISPLAY AN ASSORTMENT OF HAND-PAINTED

MINI-ORNAMENTS ON A CLEVER TRIPTYCH. OR CELEBRATE WITH A SPECIAL

ADVENT TREE. LET THE COUNTDOWN BEGIN!

How-To's on page 119

Royal Treasures

deck the halls with **jeweled** hues for a Christmas that's fit for a king. Sparkling ornaments and luxurious adornments lend a magical air of **majesty** to the season.

The first one to sneak down the stairs on Christmas morning will behold a most enchanting sight: our jolly jester doll (opposite) guarding the gifts from his regal harlequin chair. A golden tree sparkles like a fairy-tale tableau come to life, while king-size candlesticks, made of poplar or pine, give shiny tapers the royal treatment.

How-To's on page 123

TWELVE-POINT STAR

You need: Mat board; craft knife; masking tape; scissors; 20-gauge floral wire; wire cutters; glue gun; metallic gold acrylic paint; sponge brush; matte decoupage medium; gold glitter; thin metallic gold wire.

Cutting: Draw twenty-four 12"H x 2³/₄"W triangles on mat board; cut out using craft knife.

Assembling points: Cut 11" of masking tape; place one 12" floral wire lengthwise along center of sticky side, with ends overhanging evenly. Fold sticky halves of tape together to create paper selvage for wire. Make two more 11" selvages in same way. Align four triangles side by side, with bottom edges and top points even. Glue one selvage along bottom edges of triangles. Glue one triangle on top of each of the other four triangles, encasing selvage between triangles. Make two more groups, of eight triangles each, in the same way; do not trim wire tails.

Painting: Paint one side of each triangle gold; let dry. Coat with decoupage medium. Sprinkle with glitter; let dry. Apply another coat of medium; let dry. Paint other side of triangles in same manner.

Assembling star: Bend one selvage into a square, with one triangle pointing outward from each side. Twist wire tails together. Make square from another selvage in same way; do not twist wire tails together. Place diagonally and perpendicularly to first square so all points show; twist wire tails together. Make and place third square perpendicularly to others so points face out in all directions. Wrap joints where corners of squares meet with metallic gold wire; secure with glue, if needed.

How-To's continued on page 125

*S*tockings with flair! What have we here? Looks as if elves left their booties to be filled up with goodies. Festoon the mantel with a dressy organza scarf and pretty painted block candles (just brush acrylic colors across the wax). A twelve-point star twinkles from the top of an opulent tree laden with beads and velvet (above). Wrap yards of bejeweled wire or string into beautiful braided stars and beaded bells (right). Gilded reindeer and velvet cones and balls add a glint of gold. Underscore all with a luxurious silk tree skirt.

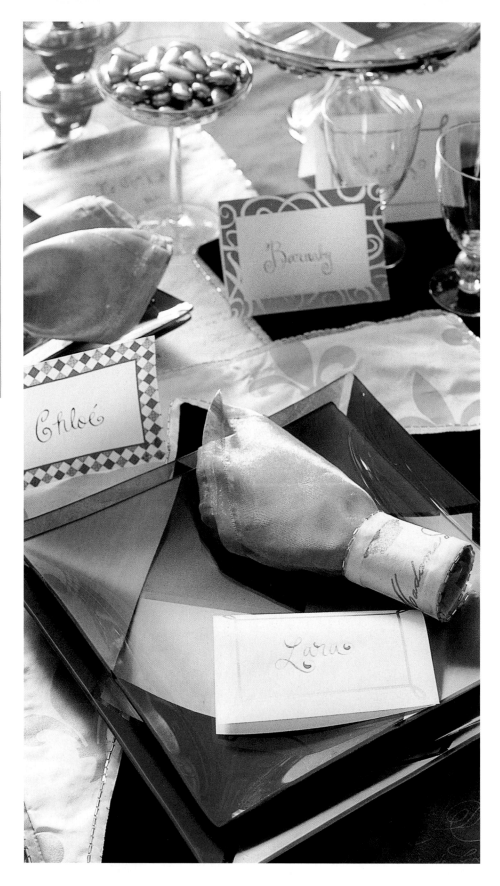

Dazzle dinner guests with fabulous hand-painted harlequin plates. Reversible purple and gold print silk and velvet place mats crisscross beneath. Roll up satiny napkins in beaded napkin rings, and pen your own holiday place cards with a gold marker. Whether served as lollipops or melt-in-your-mouth confections, jewel candies (opposite, top) are decorative as well as delectable. Bell and star cookies (opposite, bottom), made from packaged refrigerated sugar cookie dough, are fancy without the fuss.

HARLEQUIN PLATES

You need (for each): Square glass plate; masking tape; paintbrushes; glass paints in desired colors.

Painting: On wrong side of plate, apply strips of tape across each corner. Paint each corner a different color; let dry. Paint other sections of plate in same way. Follow manufacturer's directions to heat-set paints.

Note: Hand-wash plates.

SILK AND VELVET PLACE MATS

You need (for each): ¹/₂ yd each of silk and velvet fabric; 2 yds beaded trim; sewing supplies.

Cutting: From each fabric, cut one 14" x 20" piece for front and back.

Sewing: Matching raw edges, baste trim to edges of front. Pin front to back, with right sides facing and raw edges even. Stitch edges in ¹/₂" seam, leaving opening along one side. Trim corners; turn. Slipstitch opening closed.

Note: Dry-clean only.

BEADED NAPKIN RINGS

You need: Empty paper towel roll; fabric remnants in Christmas prints; craft glue; beaded trim; pins; scissors.

Making napkin rings: Cut a 3" piece of towel roll for each ring. Cut a 3¹/₂" x 4" piece of fabric for each ring. Coat roll with glue; wrap fabric around roll, right side out, so fabric extends ¹/₄" at each end. Glue fabric extensions to inside of roll. Cut beaded trim long enough to wrap around each end of each tube; glue in place to make napkin rings, holding trim in position with pins until dry.

JEWEL CANDIES

You need: ³/₄ cup water; 1¹/₂ cups sugar; ³/₄ cup light corn syrup; 2 teaspoons unsalted butter; ¹/₄ teaspoon cinnamon oil; food coloring; candy decors; colored sugar crystals; sturdy, flat sheet pans; aluminum foil; cookie cutters; vegetable cooking spray; candy thermometer.

Making candies: Line pans with foil. Place cutters on pan; spray foil and cutters with cooking spray. Mix water, sugar, corn syrup and butter in saucepan; heat over medium flame until dissolved. Increase heat; bring to boil. Cover and cook for 3 minutes. Uncover; insert candy thermometer and cook without stirring until mixture reaches 310°. Remove from heat; stir in oil and coloring. Fill cookie cutters with mixture to about ¹/₄" deep. Allow candy to cool a few minutes. Press cookie cutter into candy to cut away excess. Loosen cookie cutter and carefully push candy shape from cutter. Let cool. Lightly moisten edges with water. Dip into candy decors or sugar crystals. Allow to dry.

BELL AND STAR COOKIES

You need: 1 roll (18 ounces) refrigerated sugar cookie dough; ¹/₂ cup all-purpose flour; 1 box (16 ounces) confectioners' sugar; 3 tablespoons egg-white powder mixed with 6 tablespoons water; assorted food coloring; silver and gold dragées (see Note); pearlized edible luster dust; pure lemon extract.

Baking: Preheat oven to 350°. Knead flour into dough until smooth. Roll out dough on a lightly floured work surface to a scant ¹/₄-inch thick. Use a variety of star and bell cookie cutters to make shapes. Transfer to ungreased sheet pans and bake until golden brown, about 8 to 12 minutes. Transfer to wire racks to cool. Beat the confectioners' sugar and egg white mixture in a large bowl with an electric mixer until thick, about 4 to 5 minutes, to make frosting. Spoon 1¹/₂ cups of frosting into a pasty bag fitted with a small (#2) writing tip; cover tip and set aside. Divide remaining frosting into small batches; tint to desired colors and thin to a spreadable consistency. Coat cookies with colored frosting, adding a few dragées to some of them. Let cookies dry for at least 1 hour. Pipe white outlines on cookies, adding a few more dragées; let dry. Mix about 1 tablespoon of luster dust with 2 teaspoons of lemon extract. Using a soft paintbrush, brush luster dust over some piping and over some cookies, mixing more as needed. Makes about 1 dozen cookies.

Note: Remove dragées before eating cookies.

shimmer and shine

Create a **magical** ice palace by trimming your home in glimmering glacial hues and out-of-this-world celestial accents. It's not your ordinary Christmas décor, but a very special ethereal **vision** that's sure to enchant.

Mix up shimmery shantung, taffeta, satin and vinyl to fashion this fab foursome. On our tabletop tree (opposite), cosmic adornments — glass globes in translucent hues, swirling snowflakes and puffs of "stardust" — are coupled with more earthly trims like silver-sprayed butterflies, shiny dragonflies and birds of a feather.

How-To's on page 132

CHRISTMAS PRESENT POUCH

You need: 1 yd each of 2 coordinating silk fabrics; chalk pencil; silver paint pen; sewing supplies.

Cutting: From one fabric (main color), cut two 11" x 13" pieces for bag front and back and four 24" x 3" straps. From other fabric, cut two 11" x 16" pieces for lining front and back.

Sewing: *All stitching is done in ¼" seams, with right sides facing and raw edges even, unless noted.* Stitch lining front to bag front along one 11" edge. Stitch lining back to bag back in same way. Press lining to wrong side of bag so raw edges are even. Pin sections together, bag sides facing. Stitch each pair of straps together along long edges; turn and press. Trim one end of each strap at 45-degree angle. Insert trimmed end of each strap between sections, 4" from lower edge, with raw edges even. Stitch sides and bottom edges of bag; turn. Hand-stitch remaining ends of straps to back of bag, 2" from sides and 2" below top. Fold down cuff.

Finishing: Using paint pen, write inscription on bag.

How-To's continued on page 132

For under your evergreen, edge a diaphanous Christmas tree scarf (left) with rows of gauzy ribbons. Bring sparkle to the table by sewing shantung napkins (above) with beaded fringe to match a silk table skirt. Instead of handing out party favors, why not strap an updated Santa sack (right) onto each guest's chair? In icy blue silk, this Christmas present pouch is a gift in itself.

23

JEWELED DRAGONFLIES

You need: Metal dragonflies; fine sandpaper; antirust spray; awl; paintbrushes; acrylic paint in assorted metallic colors; acrylic glaze; jewelry glue; tweezers; small flat-back acrylic jewels.

Preparing dragonflies: Sand all surfaces lightly; apply antirust spray. Let dry. Use awl to press small, raised dots into dragonfly bodies.

Painting: Paint as desired; let dry. Coat with glaze; let dry.

Decorating: Apply glue to wings and heads (for eyes). Using tweezers, place jewels in glue; let dry.

CURLED-PAPER SNOWFLAKES

You need: White paper; craft knife; pencil; quick-drying glue; 12" of narrow ribbon; scissors.

Cutting: Cut eight 20" x $\frac{1}{2}$" (for large) or eight 10" x $\frac{1}{2}$" (for small) strips of paper.

Assembling: Fold each strip crosswise so one end is $\frac{1}{2}$" longer than the other. Wrap each end inward around pencil to curl, forming hearts. Place hearts so points meet in center. Glue sides together; let dry. Arrange curls as shown in photo. Secure with dots of glue.

Finishing: Knot ribbon ends together to form hanging loop. Slip loop through top of snowflake; pull other end of loop through.

BERIBBONED FOOTSTOOL

You need: Wood footstool; paintbrush; acrylic paint in desired color; fusible interfacing; foam core board; pins; assorted ribbons; glue gun; 1" thick piece of foam, cut to fit top of stool; heavy-duty stapler and staples; scissors.

Preparing footstool: Paint legs; let dry.

Weaving top: Measure stool top. Cut interfacing 3" larger than stool top all around. Pin interfacing, fusible side up, to foam core board. Arrange ribbons horizontally across interfacing, alternating colors and widths; pin ends to board. Weave remaining ribbons vertically through horizontal ribbons. Follow interfacing manufacturer's directions to fuse ribbons to interfacing.

Assembling: Glue foam to stool top. Center woven ribbon over foam. Wrap edges under wood seat. Staple opposite sides to underside of seat, pulling taut and smoothing ribbons from center out after each staple. Continue stapling opposite sides in same way.

How-To's continued on page 132

To cause a flutter, twist wire onto silver butterfly ornaments to wrap around the base of the champagne bucket. Teddies, especially ones like this handsome crushed-velvet bear (opposite, bottom), always deserve a seat of honor. His beribboned footstool displays a weave of satin and velvet bands in up-to-date shades. Sparkly dragonflies (opposite, top) take wing with acrylic jewels, while curled-paper snowflakes are stylized versions of the usual snipped-paper shape.

25

Here, There & Everywhere

EVERY NOOK AND CRANNY CAN HIDE A MERRY MARVEL. ADORN A MIRROR WITH FROSTY FAUX ETCHING. EMBELLISH A CHANDELIER WITH WISPY BOWS AND MISTLETOE. FASHION SENSATIONAL BEADED NAPKIN RINGS IN COOKIE-CUTTER SHAPES. GARNISH STEMWARE WITH ELEGANT TASSELS. DECK A DOOR WITH A GOODY-FILLED CONE. AND COMBINE SILVER AND GOLD STARS WITH SAND TO ANCHOR SHINING TAPERS. WHAT GLORIOUS SURPRISES!

How-To's on page 138

Holiday in White

turn your home into a winter wonderland even if there's no snow at all. Shades of white cultivate a subtle shine and set things a-shimmer from corner to corner.

A sheer, starry cloth drapes the table, and white faux flowers festoon chair backs. Even the chandelier gets a touch of fantasy from snowy blooms tucked in vials or vases. End with evocative accents like store-bought frosted trees or place cards made from heavy paper and snowflake stickers.

How-To's on page 138

With a tiered-ball topper (right), glistening ornaments and a chiffon skirt (bottom), this wondrous tree certainly says "white Christmas." The topper is easy — adorn a purchased base with sheer ribbon, pearls, feathers and rickrack. Star sequins gleam subtly on the streamers. Express the spirit of the season with magical dove and star ornaments (below and page 28) you embroider yourself.

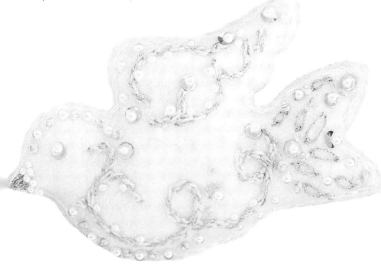

BRILLIANT BALLS

You need: Plain porcelain ball ornaments; blue, silver and white acrylic paint; paintbrushes; craft glue; glitter; metallic star stickers; acrylic jewels; ribbons; scissors.

Painting: Paint balls with desired color basecoat. When dry, add freehand details, if desired.

Finishing: As desired, apply glue to balls in desired designs. Shake glitter over glue. When dry, shake off excess glitter. Glue stickers, jewels and ribbons to balls as desired.

STAR ORNAMENTS

You need: Wooden star cutouts; silver and desired colors of acrylic paint; paintbrushes; assorted beads and sequins; craft glue.

Painting: Paint stars with desired color basecoat. When dry, add silver details by dry brushing silver across entire ornament, adding dots, or painting points of stars.

Finishing: Glue beads and sequins to stars as desired.

How-To's continued on page 138

G ive your family
bright new stockings
in a style that best
suits each person.
Coax guests with a
side table (below,
left) stocked with
tempting treats and
set with the same
stemware and linens
as your dinner table.
Sugared fruits
(bottom, right) will
add sweetness and
sparkle to your
holiday spread.

MONOGRAMMED SNOWFLAKE STOCKING

You need: 1 yd white linen for stocking and cuff; ²/₃ yd white cotton for lining; blue rayon thread (for machine embroidery) or embroidery floss (for hand embroidery); 7" of white ribbon for hanger; sewing supplies.

Cutting fabric: Enlarge pattern (page 141); add ¹/₂" seam allowance before cutting out. From linen, cut one 15¹/₂" x 7" cuff. Fold remainder of linen in half. Use pattern to cut two stockings from folded fabric. Repeat to cut two stocking linings from cotton.

Embroidering stocking front and cuff: *You may use an embroidery sewing machine and its monogram and embroidery settings/software, or you may hand embroider a monogram and snowflakes using a calligraphy book and pictures of snowflakes as guides.* Centering the largest letter 3⁵/₈" from left (short) edge of cuff, embroider monogram. Embroider snowflakes as desired on cuff and stocking front.

Stitching stocking: *When sewing, match right sides and raw edges and use a ¹/₂" seam, unless noted.* Sew stocking pieces together, leaving top edge open; clip curves. Turn. Sew lining pieces together in same manner; do not turn. Slip lining in stocking with wrong sides facing. Fold ribbon in half. With all raw edges even, pin ribbon ends to upper back edge of lining.

Adding cuff: Press under ¹/₂" on bottom (long) edge of cuff. Stitch short ends of cuff together, making a loop. Position cuff inside stocking with right side of cuff facing right side of lining. Stitch cuff to stocking. Fold cuff down over stocking.

How-To's continued on page 140

White roses are an elegant addition anywhere. Fit a silver compote with a water-soaked floral foam cone. Tuck in roses, boxwood, wax flowers and ornaments. Top with a single silver bow.

33

Accent on Easy

EVEN THE SMALLEST EFFORT CAN
RESULT IN A MAGICAL EFFECT!
FESTOON WINDOWS WITH SPLENDID
TIEBACKS. CREATE A NO-SEW
RUNNER OF VIVID RIBBONS. CAST
A COZY GLIMMER WITH PILLAR
CANDLES IN GLASS HURRICANES.
DRESS UP A MANTEL OR SHELF WITH
PAPER DOILIES, FLORAL NAPKINS
AND BEADED TRIM. TREAT POTS AND
VASES TO FANCY TRAPPINGS. VOILÁ
— INSTANT ELEGANCE!

How-To's on page 144

red, white & true Christmas

for country atmosphere with a twist, take down-home **denim** up a notch with **raw-silk** plaids and **glitzy** trims. This all-American **color** scheme is sure to give your home a warm and wonderful glow.

Create a homey, rustic appeal by setting a live tree in a wooden half-barrel. For evocative accents, hunt garage sales or your own attic for timeworn toys. Fill out the tree trimmings with a shimmering garland and plenty of purchased red, white and blue balls.

DENIM FAUX-QUILTED STOCKING

You need: Lightweight denim; raw silk plaid fabric; seam sealant; white thread; sewing supplies.

Making pattern: Enlarge stocking pattern (page 146) to 14¹/₂" tall. Add ¹/₂" all around for seam allowance. Cut out.

Cutting: *Denim* – Cut stocking front, adding 1" to top of front piece. Cut stocking front apart horizontally near top of foot. Reverse pattern and cut stocking back following pattern. ***Raw silk plaid*** – Cut a 1¹/₄"W bias strip the same length as horizontal cut. Cut another 1¹/₄"W plaid bias strip same length as from tip of toe to top of stocking. Cut one oval and one circle to fit on upper front stocking piece. Apply seam sealant along edges of oval and circle. Cut a 2"W x 6"H strip for hanging loop.

Sewing: *All stitching is done in ¹/₂" seams, with right sides facing and raw edges even, unless noted.* Topstitch diagonal lines across lower part of stocking front. Position oval and circle on upper part of stocking front; zigzag stitch around edges to secure. With wrong sides together, press bias strips in half lengthwise. Pin short bias strip along lower front stocking piece. Sew lower and upper section of stocking front together. Pin long bias strip around edge of stocking front. Sew stocking front and back together, leaving top edge open. Clip curves; turn. To hem, fold top edge under ¹/₄", then ¹/₄" again; stitch in place close to fold.

Finishing: Fold hanging loop strip in half lengthwise; sew long edges together. Turn. Fold strip in half to form loop. Stitch ends to upper back corner of stocking.

How-To's continued on page 144

Combine durable denim with assorted trims and pieces of plaid in exciting new Christmas stockings (left) for your family. Tie festive accents onto chair backs (above, right). To do, wind a faux-berry vine around a small grapevine wreath and hang a sweet plaid heart in the center. Cover your holiday table with a tiered tablecloth (right). For complementary place mats, buy denim ones and sew or glue on sequin-trimmed plaid pockets to hold sets of flatware. Trim a birdhouse with ornaments and vines for an eye-catching centerpiece. Strips of sequin trim along the edge of the roof suggest the shimmer of icicles, while drawing the piece into the overall décor.

39

BEADED BIRD ORNAMENTS

You need: White cotton fabric; blue chambray fabric; fabric glue; silver beads; fiberfill stuffing; silver embroidery thread; sewing supplies.

Cutting: Enlarge bird and wing patterns (page 147) to desired size; add ¹/₂" all around for seams. Fold fabrics in half. Cut two birds from white fabric and two wings from blue or white fabric for each ornament.

Sewing: With right sides facing, sew birds and wings together, leaving opening for turning. Clip curves; turn. Stuff bird only with fiberfill. Slipstitch openings closed. Sew silver beads onto bird and wing to add details. Glue wing on bird. Knot ends of a 6" length of silver thread together; sew to back of ornament for hanger.

PLAID HEART ORNAMENTS

You need: Remnants of plaid raw silk fabric; fiberfill stuffing; string sequin trim; fabric glue; gold embroidery thread; sewing supplies.

To do: Enlarge heart pattern (page 145) to desired size; add ¹/₂" all around for seams. Cut two hearts from plaid. With right sides facing, sew hearts together, leaving an opening for turning. Clip curves; turn. Stuff with fiberfill. Slipstitch opening closed. Glue a length of sequin trim to heart front in shape of heart. Knot ends of a 6" length of gold thread together; sew to back of ornament for hanger.

How-To's continued on page 148

CANDY CANE ORNAMENTS

You need: Cardboard; string sequin trim – white, red; glue gun; gold embroidery thread; scissors.

To do each: Enlarge candy cane pattern (page 147) to desired size; cut out. Cut candy cane from cardboard. Glue end of white sequins to back of cardboard shape. Wrap sequins around cardboard, covering completely and gluing as needed. Glue end to back of shape. Glue red sequins over white sequins to form stripes. Knot ends of a 6" length of gold thread together; glue to back of ornament for hanger.

Mix solids and plaids with shimmery sequins in our star tree topper (above). *Transform a blue chambray pillowcase into a Santa sack (right). Just add a plaid, sequin-edged border and hem at the top to provide a casing for a cord to pull the sack closed. Make cheery ornaments like a colorful ball, a glittery heart, a beaded bird and a candy cane (opposite) in no time at all!*

frosty Touches
Take the décor outdoors

CREATE YOUR OWN WINTER WONDERLAND IN A TWINKLING! FILL
FANCIFUL BOOTS WITH FRESH GREENS AND STARS-ON-A-STICK. TRIM TREES
WITH ICY STARS. LIGHT UP YOUR WALK WITH A HALO OF HANGING LAMPS.
STRING WOODEN STARS WITH TINY WHITE LIGHTS. DECORATE A CHILD'S
CHAIR WITH A STAR SUN-CATCHER. HOW MAGICAL!

How-To's on page 149

43

MERRY

mini trees

Shake up your seasonal routine with a tiny tree tailored to your personal style. Go sleek and modern, **gracefully** elegant or casually humorous. Friends and family will take delight in your **magnificent** miniature.

Silver reindeer leap across white bristle branches in this gleaming tree. Note the paper fortunes hung with care and the shiny bells and pinecones arranged around the base. For a gorgeous edible accent (opposite), use wooden picks to hang fresh fruits on a plastic-wrapped foam cone. Embellish with fancy ribbon and petite bows. Fantastic!

GOLDEN WIRE TREE

You need: Gold wire tree; wire cutters; gold 20-gauge wire; gold crimp beads; assorted glass beads (sizes 10/0, 6/0); pliers (flat-nose, round-nose); carrot; gold ribbon; 7"-dia painted terra-cotta pot; glass heart charms; gold metal bells; glass star (topper).

Preparing tree: Cut off every other branch. Unfurl others to add length.

Making beaded ornaments: *Spirals* – Cut 15"L wire. Slip a crimp bead ¹/₂" from one end; crimp closed with flat-nose pliers. Slip on eight beads; add crimp bead; crimp closed. Repeat at 1" intervals until complete. Shape spiral using round-nose pliers; loop end for hanger. *Icicles* – Make same as spirals, using carrot to shape icicle.

Finishing: Glue ribbon around pot. Glue ribbon bow on pot. Set tree in pot. Hang all ornaments; tie on ribbon bows. Wire star to treetop.

A painted branch (above) gets royal treatment with red birds, balls, even marbles atop a red vase. Brightly colored terra-cotta wrapped in ribbon is the base for a golden wire tree (right) decorated in miniature glass hearts, bells and beaded ornaments.

*T*wig clotheslines and wee clothespins hold pint-size mittens and pj's on this clever tree (right), while a child's pom-pom hat and kilt skirt dress up the top and bottom. Pamper your pet with his own Christmas tree (below). Dress up photo frame ornaments with paint and pet-motif buttons. Make paper pictures by covering a cardboard circle with pet-patterned wrapping paper, then trim the ornament with cording, sequins and ribbon. Finish with a doghouse topper and stenciled tree skirt. Paws-itively perfect!

DOGHOUSE TOPPER

You need: 5^1/$_4$"W x 6"L piece of ^{1}/$_4$" plywood; 5" x 4" piece of ^{1}/$_8$" plywood; saber saw; sandpaper; glue; paintbrushes; acrylic paint – yellow, black, white, green, assorted colors; dog biscuit; ^{1}/$_8$"W red ribbon; ^{1}/$_2$"dia. jingle bell; 3" of elastic cord; glue gun; pet photo; scissors.

Cutting wood: Enlarge doghouse pattern (page 150); cut out. Trace doghouse pattern onto ^{1}/$_4$" plywood; cut out. From ^{1}/$_8$" plywood, cut a 3"W x 4"L back, one ^{1}/$_2$"W x 3^5/$_8$"L roof piece and one ^{1}/$_2$"W x 3^1/$_2$"L roof piece.

Assembling: Glue roof pieces to house, with overhang at front and sides.

Painting: Paint roof red. Paint doghouse yellow with white arch; let dry. Add brush strokes of bright colors. Add black stripes to arch. Paint dog biscuit green with white dots.

Finishing: Tie bell to biscuit with ribbon; glue above door. With wood glue, attach backing. Trim photo to fit door opening; glue. Hot-glue ends of elastic to back for hanger.

PAW PRINT TREE SKIRT

Size: 20"W x 50"L

You need: ^{2}/$_3$ yd of 60"W cotton canvas; sewing supplies; 4^1/$_2$ yds red jumbo rickrack; blank stencil sheet; black marker; craft knife; stencil brush; brown fabric paint.

Making skirt: Cut canvas 23"W x 53"L. Hem by turning under edges ^{1}/$_2$", then 1"; stitch. Stitch rickrack around all edges.

Stenciling: Use paw print pattern (page 150) to make two stencils – use as-is for small paw print; enlarge for large print. Trace designs onto stencil sheet; cut out. Stencil paw prints across skirt.

4 takes on tradition

fill the tree with your most **treasured** trims, then pull everything together with a delightful **unifying** theme.

Beautiful bundles of dried or silk flowers lend even mismatched ornaments a touch of class. We used dried roses and hydrangeas, held together and hung with satin ribbon. A mix of muted tones is understated, but go bold if you like — or all white for a more formal feeling.

The usual baubles take on a storybook quality when linked by charming bear cookies. Momma, Poppa and the kids — all dressed in their Sunday best — are cute and easy to make. Mix up your favorite gingerbread batter, then create the shapes with different-size bear cutters. Before baking, use a wooden skewer to form a hole for hanging. When done, let cookies cool completely while you whip up various shades of royal icing (see page 87). With icing, clothe bears as desired. If necessary, repoke holes before threading with thin ribbon.

49

A planned palette can organize any tree in sublime style. Buy ornaments, garlands, lights, whatever, in your chosen color; even simple ribbon bows can be enlisted to fill out empty spaces. You'll be amazed at how things fall into place, with the main shade highlighting complementary colors and little details.

50

Handmade star ornaments sprinkled among your varied collection set a glorious tone. Simply use gold paint to dress up wooden pinch-type clothespins and large store-bought wooden stars. Paint small self-adhering stars green and outline with green glitter glue; center on large stars and stick on. Hot-glue to clothespin.

FUN! for kids

LET SANTA'S LITTLEST HELPERS LEND A HAND WITH EASY CHRISTMAS CRAFTS! CREATE A CLEVER WREATH OF KIDS' HANDPRINTS. KEEP BUSY ELVES HAPPY WITH EDIBLE ORNAMENTS. STRING TOGETHER A BRIGHT HOLIDAY GARLAND. RING IN THE SEASON WITH A JOLLY SANTA BELL. BUILD A FUN SNOWFRIEND TABLE TOPPER FOR A JOYFUL MEMORY THAT WILL LAST A LIFETIME.

Snowballs 5¢

How-To's on page 150

53

Gifts Galore

One-of-a-kind, handmade gifts are sure to bring **smiles** on Christmas morning. After all, "from me to you" is even more meaningful when what's inside the wrapping is something you crafted yourself.

This soft, fuzzy chill-chaser set is sure to get a warm reception. The 72-inch teal scarf sports hand pockets in moss-green — a perfect match to the jaunty, pointed cap. A bright and bold toddler tam (opposite, from top) keeps Jack Frost from nipping. Gorgeous shadings lend this mohair artwork tote its intriguing appeal. Dad and son vests feature a cable design, rolled collars and zipper necks.

CHILL-CHASER SCARF AND HAT

Scarf: 11"W x 72"L

Hat: 20" around

You need: Bulky weight, fuzzy textured yarn, 1³/₄ oz/50g balls: *Scarf* – 4 balls in teal blue (A) and 1 ball in olive green (B); size 10 (6mm) needles or size needed to obtain gauge. **Hat** – 1 ball in olive green (B); size 10 (6mm) circular needles, 16"L. **Both** – Pins; yarn needle; stitch marker.

Knit abbreviations: Listed on page 156.

Gauge (for both): 12 sts and 20 rows = 4" in St st. TAKE TIME TO CHECK GAUGE.

Scarf: With A, cast on 32 sts. Work in garter st (knit every row) until piece measures 72". Bind off.

Scarf pocket (make 2): With B, cast on 18 sts. Work in St st until piece measures 6". Knit 7 rows. Bind off.

Scarf finishing: With RS facing and garter st trim facing upwards, pin pocket to scarf about 2" above end and 2" from each side edge of scarf. With yarn needle and B, sew pocket to scarf. Sew second pocket to other end of scarf.

Hat: With circular needle and B, cast on 60 sts. Place marker on right needle tip to mark beginning of rnd (sl marker every rnd). Being careful that stitches aren't twisted on needle, join rnd and work in St st (knit every rnd) until piece measures 7". Shape crown in rows as follows, turning at end of each row and purling WS rows: *Row 1 (RS)* – (K8, k2tog) 6 times – 54 sts. *Row 3* – (K7, k2tog) 6 times – 48 sts. *Row 5* – (K6, k2tog) 6 times – 42 sts. Cont to dec 6 sts every RS row in this manner until 12 sts remain. *Next RS Row* – (K2tog) 6 times. *Next WS Row* – P across 6 sts. *Next RS Row* – (K2tog) 3 times. Make point in I-cord on rem 3 sts as follows: Do not turn at end of row. Instead, slip sts to opposite end of circular needle, pull yarn around back and knit every row. Work until cord measures 1". K3 tog. Fasten off. With yarn needle, pull yarn end through center of I-cord to conceal.

Hat finishing: With yarn needle and B, sew hat closed at seam along the shaping rows of the crown.

How-To's continued on page 153

BUTTON PEOPLE

You need (for each): Two 2' lengths of narrow elastic cord; about 75-80 assorted flat-back buttons.

Making hat/head/body: Fold one cord in half. String one medium button onto cord, passing cord through opposite holes in button. Push button to fold. String two medium, then one large button onto cords in same way. String two medium, then two small buttons to make face and neck. String five large, then two medium buttons to make chest and waist. String three large, then two medium buttons to make hips and tops of legs.

Making legs: Separate cord halves. String 13 medium and two small buttons on each half. Pass each cord end through opposite holes in last button and back through buttons; knot ends together securely at top of first leg button.

Making arms: Pass remaining cord between previously strung cords, just below neck buttons. String 12 small buttons on each side to make arms. Secure cord ends same as for legs.

Note: Button people are not intended for children younger than 3 years of age.

SQUARE-IN-SQUARE SNUGGLE PILLOW

You need: Fleece fabrics – 1/2 yd in main color, 8" x 8" square contrasting color; embroidery needle; embroidery floss in contrasting colors; sewing supplies; 15" x 15" square pillow form.

Cutting: From main color fleece, cut one 17" square front and two 17" x 12" back sections.

Making pillow front: Pin contrasting square in center of front piece, right side up. Sew to front piece with blanket stitches using contrasting floss. Sew a cross-stitch in each corner of center square.

Assembling pillow: *All stitching is done with 1/2" seams and right sides facing, unless noted.* Turn under 1/2", then 1", on one long edge of each back section; press. Stitch close to fold to form hem. Overlap hemmed edges 4", with right sides up and raw edges even; baste at overlap to form back. Stitch front to back. Trim seams; turn.

Finishing: Sew blanket stitches around pillow edges using contrasting floss. Insert pillow form into cover.

CHECKERBOARD SNUGGLE PILLOW

You need: Fleece fabrics – 1/2 yd main color, one 9" square each of 3 contrasting colors; sewing supplies; embroidery needle; embroidery floss in contrasting colors; 15" x 15" square pillow form.

Cutting: From main color fleece, cut one 9" square for front and two 17" x 12" pieces for back sections.

Making pillow front: *All stitching is done with 1/2" seams and right sides facing, unless noted.* Sew two 9" squares together along one edge; unfold. Repeat with remaining squares. Sew sections together along one long edge; unfold to form pillow front.

Assembling pillow: Turn under 1/2", then 1", on one long edge of each back section; press. Stitch close to fold to form hem. Overlap hemmed edges 4", with right sides up and raw edges even; baste at overlap to form back. Stitch front to back. Trim seams; turn.

Finishing: Sew blanket stitches around pillow edges using contrasting floss. Insert pillow form into cover.

Kids will get a kick out of wacky button people, so raid your sewing kit for elastic cord and buttons in all colors and sizes. Blanket stitching gives square-in-a-square and checkered pillows (top) an edge. It's hip to be square!

DISTRESSED RIBBON FRAMES

You need (for each): Unfinished wooden picture frame; paintbrushes; acrylic paint; sandpaper; sealer; ribbon; scissors; low-temp glue gun; 4 buttons.

To do: Sand frame. Paint frame; let dry. Sand all edges for aged look. Apply sealer; let dry. Glue lengths of ribbon to front of frame. Glue buttons to corners.

PATRIOT'S MIRROR

You need: Unfinished wooden picture frame; wood stars; paintbrushes; acrylic paints – red, white, blue; sandpaper; sealer; hammer; nails; mirror, cut to fit frame.

Painting: Sand frame and stars. Paint frame and stars in assorted colors; let dry. Sand all edges for aged look. Apply sealer; let dry.

Assembling: Nail stars around edge of frame. Mount mirror in frame.

How-To's continued on page 154

Classy redwork adds a nostalgic touch to this sweet and simple American quilt (left). Our patriot's mirror (above) is a star-studded vision — and it's a breeze to make. For a wonderfully sentimental gift, include a favorite photo with a distressed ribbon frame (top).

GILDED PLATES

You need: Clear glass plates; desired motifs, cut from wrapping paper; paintbrushes; decoupage medium; acrylic paints – gold, desired contrast color; gold leaf adhesive; gold leaf; soft brush.

Decoupaging: Brush decoupage medium onto right side of motif; press onto underside of plate. Let dry.

Painting: Working on underside of plate, paint outer band of plate and outer edge of center section in contrast color paint; let dry. Paint center section of plate gold; let dry.

Applying leaf: Brush gold leaf adhesive on unpainted area of underside of plate. Let dry until tacky, following manufacturer's instructions. Press leaf into adhesive; burnish with fingers. Using soft brush, remove excess leaf. Let dry.

Finishing: Apply three coats of decoupage medium to underside of plate, letting dry after each coat.

Please a literary type with jumbo "A to Z" bookends. The initials are actually cardboard wrapped in cheesecloth for bulk! A tea lover will be charmed by these decorative gilded plates (top), but you can change the decoupage motif to suit anyone on your list.

WOODEN PLACE MATS

You need (for each): Wood – 12" x 16" piece of ¼" birch plywood, 12" x 16" piece of thin beadboard paneling, 56" of ⅜" wood trim; saw; miter box; wood glue; phone books or other weights; masking tape; paintbrushes; primer; sandpaper; acrylic paints – light and dark shades of main color, gold, white; rag; decoupage medium; color photocopies of vintage greeting cards; scissors; varnish.

Laminating wood: Apply a thin coat of glue to plywood; adhere to wrong side of paneling (be sure edges are even). Weight assembly with phone books; let glue set overnight.

Adding trim: Cut trim, mitering corners, to fit sides of place mat; glue to edges. Secure with masking tape until set. Remove tape.

Painting: Prime; when dry, sand. Apply two coats of lighter shade of paint, then paint on alternating darker stripes. Rub on a thin coat of gold along trim; wipe off excess with rag.

Decoupaging: Cut motifs from photocopies; brush decoupage medium on wrong side. Adhere to mat; let dry. Brush motifs with decoupage medium.

Finishing: Polka-dot "snowflakes" in white paint on alternating stripes. When dry, apply several coats of varnish.

How-To's continued on page 155

MOSAIC FRAME

You need: Unfinished wooden picture frame; paintbrush; acrylic paint; decoupage paper, or other heavyweight, shiny paper in assorted colors; scissors; foam paintbrush; decoupage medium; clear acrylic glaze.

To do: Paint frame; let dry. Cut paper into small squares. Arrange squares on frame into desired design, cutting pieces to fit as needed. Working on one small area at a time, remove squares from area, brush decoupage medium onto area, then press squares into medium. Continue in same manner until all squares are glued in place; let dry. Brush frame with glaze; let dry.

Your favorite shutterbug will welcome fanciful stamped and mosaic photo frames. Wood-paneled place mats (top) *add a touch of whimsy to the Yuletide table.*

An exquisite hostess gift: vintage wooden spools become clever Christmas candlesticks with a sprig of holly and a few berries. Delight an old-fashioned friend with beribboned fruit in "timeworn" pots (top). An appliquéd basket of posies in muted shades makes this dreamy pillow (opposite, from top) bloom. With simple beads and rich ribbon, this keepsake frame is an elegant ornament. Surprise someone special with a long-forgotten treasure: stuffed with holiday greens, this beloved ice skate promises to conjure favorite Christmas memories.

FRUITFUL OFFERINGS

You need (for each): Terra-cotta pot and saucer; acrylic paints – green, rust; paintbrush; sandpaper; fresh fruit; assorted ribbons; mini artificial greenery garland.

Painting pot: Paint pot one color; paint saucer the other color. Let dry. Sand all edges for aged look.

Finishing: Wrap ribbon or garland around fruits to resemble "gift-packages." Place pot in saucer. Arrange fruits in pot.

CHARMING CANDLESTICKS

You need: Antique thread spools; artificial berries and greenery; low-temp glue gun; narrow ribbon; taper candles to fit spools.

To do: Glue berries and greenery to spools. Tie ribbon bows on spools as desired. Insert tapers into candlesticks.

Note: Never leave burning candles unattended.

FOLKSY APPLIQUÉD PILLOW

Size: 14" x 18"

You need: Freezer paper; wool fabric – 15" x 19" brown, 9" x 11" black, 9" x 8" ecru, two $1^1/4$" x 9" strips plaid, scraps of 2 greens, brown, rust, yellow and orange; 15" x 19" flannel backing; embroidery floss – red, black; embroidery needle; twelve 3mm black beads; 6 buttons; sewing supplies; fiberfill stuffing.

Making patterns: Enlarge patterns (page 155). Trace following patterns onto freezer paper – one basket, five leaves, one tulip, one posy. Trace six $1/2$" to $1^1/4$" circles for three flowers and three centers. Cut out pieces.

Cutting appliqués: Set iron for wool. Press patterns (shiny side down) on right side of wool; paper will adhere. Cut out. Cut four $3/8$"W x 4"L stems.

Appliquéing top: *Embroidery diagrams are on page 156.* Center basket on black wool; pin. Appliqué basket with red floss, leaving rim unstitched. Tuck stems in; pin. Appliqué stems with black floss. In red, finish rim and appliqué handle with long stitches and quilt basket on dash lines. In black, appliqué flowers and leaves on stems. Sew beads at X's.

Piecing: Center top on brown wool; pin. Pin plaid strips against panel sides. Stitch with black floss whipstitches. Sew buttons on strips.

Finishing: Pin top to back, right sides facing. Sew together using a $1/2$" seam, leaving an opening for turning. Turn and stuff; sew closed.

KEEPSAKE FRAME

You need: Two 4" x 4" pieces of cardboard; 4" x 4" piece of felt; craft glue; photo; ribbon – 1 yd of 3mm gold metallic, 18" of 15mm rust metallic, 16" of 32mm rust ruffle; nineteen 5mm gold beads; scissors.

Preparing frame and backing: Cut a 3" x 3" square from center of one cardboard piece for frame. Glue photo to center of remaining cardboard for backing.

Adding ribbons: Cut four 4" lengths each of rust ruffle and rust metallic ribbons. Glue the metallic ribbon (centered) on top of each ruffle piece. Trim the ends of each length in 45° angle for mitered corners. Glue the ribbons to the frame, mitered corners matching. Glue the beads around the edges of the frame (save three for hanging loop.)

Assembling: Glue felt to back of cardboard backing. Cut a 20" length of gold ribbon for hanging loop. Glue the ends of the ribbon to the top of cardboard side of backing, $1/2$" in from each side. Loop ribbon in center, making a "bow"; glue overlaps to secure. Glue three beads at overlap. Glue backing and frame together, sandwiching photo in between. Glue remaining gold ribbon around side edges of cardboard.

Palate-Pleasing Presents

Call us **old-fashioned**, but we still think homemade goodies are the best gifts. Packed and presented with a **flourish**, they're a lovely way to show your appreciation to a helpful neighbor, a **favorite** co-worker or a gracious hostess.

GINGER STARS

- $1/2$ cup (1 stick) unsalted butter, at room temperature
- $1/2$ cup granulated sugar
- 1 egg
- $1/4$ cup light molasses
- 2 cups all-purpose flour
- 1 tablespoon ground ginger
- 1 teaspoon baking soda
- $1/4$ cup crystallized ginger, chopped
- Coarse sugar, for decorating

1. Beat together butter and granulated sugar in a medium-size bowl until smooth and creamy. Beat in egg and molasses.
2. Combine flour, ground ginger, baking soda and crystallized ginger in food processor. Process until pieces of crystallized ginger are no longer visible. Stir into butter mixture. Divide dough in half; wrap each half in plastic wrap; refrigerate 1 hour.
3. Heat oven to 350°. On lightly floured surface or between 2 sheets of plastic wrap, roll half of dough to $1/8$- to $1/4$-inch thickness. Refrigerate rolled dough again until firm, for 10 to 15 minutes.
4. Cut out stars with 2- to 3-inch cookie cutters. Place cookies on ungreased baking sheets. Gather together scraps, refrigerate and reroll for more cookies. Decorate tops with coarse sugar. Repeat with the remaining half of dough.
5. Bake cookies in 350° oven for 10 minutes or until lightly browned around edges. Transfer cookies to wire racks to cool completely. Store in airtight container.
Yield: $2^1/2$ dozen 2-inch stars and 2 dozen 3-inch stars.

MELTAWAYS

- 1 cup (2 sticks) unsalted butter, at room temperature
- 1 cup confectioners' sugar
- 2 teaspoons vanilla
- 2 cups all-purpose flour
- 1 cup finely ground pecans
- 1 cup confectioners' sugar, for dusting

1. Beat together butter and 1 cup confectioners' sugar in bowl until smooth and creamy. Add vanilla.
2. On low speed of an electric mixer, beat in flour and nuts. Wrap dough in plastic wrap; refrigerate until firm, for 1 to 2 hours.
3. Heat oven to 325°. Pinch off pieces of dough in rounded teaspoonfuls. Roll into logs. Taper ends; bend into crescents. Place on ungreased baking sheets.
4. Bake in 325° oven for 19 to 20 minutes, until lightly browned.
5. Transfer cookies to wire rack. Sprinkle heavily with confectioners' sugar. Cool completely. Sprinkle again with confectioners' sugar. Store in airtight container.
Yield: $4^1/2$ dozen.

CHOCOLATE-COVERED CHERRY COOKIES

- $3/4$ cup all-purpose flour
- 1 tube (18 ounces) refrigerated sugar cookie dough
- 2 jars (10 ounces each) maraschino cherries with stems
- 18 ounces semisweet chocolate

1. Heat oven to 350°.
2. Knead flour into cookie dough.
3. Drain cherries; blot dry with paper toweling. Wrap each cherry in 1 teaspoon dough; wrap the stem in aluminum foil. Repeat using all dough and cherries. Place cherries 1 inch apart on ungreased baking sheet. Bake 14 minutes or until firm; cool on wire rack.
4. Melt chocolate. Dip cherries into chocolate; do not coat stems. Let set up, about 30 minutes. Store in airtight container in a cool place.
Yield: 4 dozen.

Moon-shaped Meltaways and tasty Ginger Stars (opposite) *are simply heavenly — they practically melt in your mouth! Chocolate-Covered Cherry Cookies (not pictured) are easy gifts for the chocoholics in your life.*

FILLED CANDY-CANE COFFEECAKE

Frozen bread dough, which can be purchased in packages of 3 loaves, may be substituted; if so, begin the recipe at Step 2.

Dough:
- 2 envelopes active dry yeast
- 1/2 cup warm water
- 1 1/4 cups buttermilk
- 3/4 cup granulated sugar
- 1/2 cup (1 stick) butter or margarine, at room temperature
- 2 eggs
- 1 1/2 teaspoons baking powder
- 2 teaspoons salt
- 6 cups all-purpose flour

Filling:
- 1 package (6 ounces) dried mixed fruit bits
- 1/2 cup walnut pieces
- 2 tablespoons butter or margarine, melted
- 1 1/2 teaspoons ground cinnamon

Glaze:
- 1 cup confectioners' sugar
- 1 tablespoon water
- Red maraschino cherries, halved, for garnish (optional)

1. Prepare Dough: Coat baking sheet with nonstick vegetable-oil cooking spray. Dissolve yeast in water in large mixing bowl. Add buttermilk, sugar, butter, eggs, baking powder, salt and 2 cups flour. Beat on medium speed of an electric mixer for 2 minutes. Stir in remaining flour by hand. Turn dough out onto well-floured surface; knead 5 minutes or until smooth and elastic. Divide into thirds.

2. Roll each third of dough out into a 15 x 6-inch rectangle. Place on prepared baking sheet. On long sides of rectangles, make 2-inch cuts, perpendicular to edge, at 1/2-inch intervals.

3. Prepare Filling: Combine mixed fruit, walnuts, butter and cinnamon in small bowl. Spoon one-third of filling lengthwise down center of each rectangle. Fold over strips; pinch the open ends along one side to seal. Shape each into a cane. Cover breads with a clean kitchen towel; let rise in warm place, away from drafts, until doubled, about 45 minutes.

4. Heat oven to 375°.

5. Bake coffeecakes in 375° oven for 18 to 20 minutes or until golden. Cool on wire racks. Glaze coffeecakes; garnish with cherry halves.

Yield: 3 coffeecakes (8 servings each).

Make-Ahead Tip: To freeze coffeecakes, bake cakes as described in recipe, but do not glaze. Cool completely on wire racks. Wrap tightly in plastic wrap, then aluminum foil. Freeze for up to 2 months. To serve, thaw completely, then reheat in 350° oven about 15 minutes. Glaze while still hot. Decorate with cherries.

Maraschino cherries become scrumptious red stripes on this Filled Candy-Cane Coffeecake, but the real treat is the fruity surprise nestled inside.

SOUTH-OF-THE-BORDER SNACK MIX

    4   cups broken tortilla chips
          (bite-size pieces)
    3   cups multi-bran cereal squares
    2   cups cheese tidbits
    2   cups mini pretzel twists
1 1/2   cups dry-roasted unsalted peanuts
  1/4   cup (1/2 stick) butter or
          margarine, melted
    2   tablespoons Worcestershire sauce
    1   tablespoon chili powder
    2   teaspoons ground cumin
    1   teaspoon garlic powder
    1   teaspoon seasoned salt
    1   teaspoon ground red pepper
          (cayenne), or to taste

1. Position oven racks on second and third levels in oven. Heat oven to 250°.
2. Toss together tortilla chip pieces, cereal, cheese tidbits, pretzels and peanuts in a large bowl until well mixed.
3. Stir together the melted butter, Worcestershire sauce, chili powder, cumin, garlic powder, seasoned salt and ground red pepper in a small bowl until well mixed. Pour seasoning mixture over snack mix, tossing until the mix is lightly and evenly moistened with the seasoning mixture. Pour the snack mix into two ungreased 15 x 10 x 1-inch jelly-roll pans.
4. Bake snack mix in 250° oven for 30 minutes or until coating on the snack mix begins to darken slightly; stir snack mix every 10 minutes, turning and reversing the jelly-roll pans halfway through the baking. Let the snack mix cool completely in pans on wire racks. Store in airtight container.
Yield: About 12 1/2 cups.

*H*appiness by the handful is a glass container brimming with chili-powder-laced South-of-the-Border Snack Mix or Almonds Italiano touched with basil and thyme.

ALMONDS ITALIANO

    2   tablespoons olive oil
    1   egg white
    2   teaspoons dried basil
    2   teaspoons dried oregano
    2   teaspoons dried rosemary
    2   teaspoons dried thyme
    2   teaspoons garlic powder
    2   teaspoons onion powder
  1/2   teaspoon salt
    3   cups (about 14 ounces) whole
          unblanched almonds

1. Heat oven to 275°.
2. Whisk together olive oil, egg white, basil, oregano, rosemary, thyme, garlic powder, onion powder and salt in a large bowl. Add the almonds, 1 cup at a time, stirring well after each addition, until almonds are evenly coated with herb mixture. Pour into a 15 x 10 x 1-inch jelly-roll pan.
3. Bake in 275° oven for 45 minutes or until the almonds are lightly toasted, stirring every 10 minutes. Let almonds cool completely. Store in airtight container.
Yield: 3 cups.

Light-years ahead of kiddie carnival fare, these fanciful Caramel Apples are accented with melted chocolate and pistachios. When set, lay each atop a cupcake liner. You'll go nutty for our Sugar & Spice Nuts (not pictured) — a hearty mixture of almonds, pecans, walnuts, cashews and peanuts, tossed in a sugary coating.

SUGAR & SPICE NUTS
Bring to a holiday fete as a party favor.

- 2 egg whites
- 1 cup whole almonds
- 1 cup pecan halves
- 1 cup walnut halves
- 1 cup cashews
- 1 cup peanuts
- 1/2 cup sugar
- 2 teaspoons ground cinnamon
- 1/4 teaspoon ground allspice
- 1/8 teaspoon ground nutmeg

1. Heat oven to 375°. Grease a 15 x 10 x 1-inch jelly-roll pan.
2. Beat egg whites in a large bowl until very frothy. Stir in almonds, pecans, walnuts, cashews, peanuts, 1/4 cup sugar, cinnamon, allspice and nutmeg; toss until nuts are evenly coated. Spread nuts in an even layer in prepared jelly-roll pan.
3. Bake in 375° oven for 10 minutes or until coating is partially set. Add remaining 1/4 cup sugar to the pan, stirring until the nuts are well coated. Bake 10 minutes longer or until nuts are golden brown. Transfer pan to a wire rack to cool completely.
4. Store nuts in airtight container at cool room temperature for up to 1 month.
Yield: 5 cups.

CARAMEL APPLES

- 1 piece plastic foam sheet (about 18 x 7 inches)
- 8 small to medium-size McIntosh apples (about 3 1/2 pounds total)
- 8 wooden ice-cream sticks OR long cinnamon sticks
- 2 packages (14 ounces each) creamy caramels (total of 98 candies)
- 2 tablespoons water
- 3/4 cup shelled pistachios, coarsely chopped
- 1/2 cup semisweet chocolate chips

1. Place foam sheet on a flat surface. Lightly coat large baking sheet with nonstick vegetable-oil cooking spray.
2. Remove stems from apples; wash and dry apples. Insert wooden stick or cinnamon stick into stem end of each apple.
3. Place unwrapped caramels in medium-size saucepan. Add water; heat over medium-low heat, stirring occasionally, until caramels are melted and smooth.

4. Working quickly with one apple at a time, and keeping caramel over low heat, dip the apple into caramel, turning to coat apple completely; remove the apple from caramel and gently shake, letting excess caramel drip back into saucepan. Pat pistachios onto top of apple and 1 inch down sides; place on prepared sheet. Refrigerate 10 minutes or until caramel is cool.
5. Meanwhile, heat chocolate chips in top of double boiler over hot, not boiling, water until melted and smooth. Drizzle chocolate on top of apples. Press wooden sticks or cinnamon sticks into foam. Remove remaining chocolate from heat. Refrigerate apples until the chocolate hardens, about 1 hour. Transfer from foam sheet to foil cupcake liners. Reheat chocolate and drizzle decorations onto apples. Be sure your gift recipients know the cinnamon sticks are non-edible.
Yield: 8 apples.

CHUNKY TOMATO SAUCE

- 2 tablespoons olive oil
- 1 cup chopped onion
- 2 cloves garlic, finely chopped
- 1 cup chopped sweet green pepper
- 1 cup chopped zucchini
- 1 cup chopped mushrooms (about 2 ounces)
- 3 canned flat anchovies, chopped
- 2 cans (28 ounces each) chopped tomatoes
- 1 can (6 ounces) tomato paste
- $1/2$ teaspoon sugar
- $1/4$ cup chopped parsley
- 1 tablespoon balsamic vinegar
- 1 tablespoon salt
- $1/2$ teaspoon black pepper

1. Heat olive oil in 4-quart saucepan over medium-high heat. Add onion and garlic; sauté 8 minutes or until almost tender. Add green pepper, zucchini, mushrooms and anchovies; sauté for 8 to 10 minutes or until vegetables are almost tender.

2. Stir in chopped tomatoes, tomato paste and sugar. Bring to boiling. Reduce heat to low; simmer, uncovered, 30 minutes or until thickened, stirring occasionally. Stir in parsley, vinegar, salt and pepper.

3. Spoon sauce into 2 sterilized 1-quart canning jars; seal. Cool slightly on wire racks. Refrigerate for up to 2 weeks.

Yield: 2 quarts.

Just call this a tantalizing tribute to Italy. Arrange a jar of our Chunky Tomato Sauce with pasta, Parmesan cheese and a grater in a colander. (Keep sauce and cheese in fridge until the last minute, then add to the cache.) Snappy Ginger Jellies (above, right) are tossed in sugar for a sweet, snowy coating.

GINGER JELLIES

- 1 jar (23 ounces) unsweetened applesauce
- 2 tablespoons grated fresh gingerroot
- $1^1/2$ cups sugar plus $1/3$ cup, for coating
- $1/8$ teaspoon salt
- 1 tablespoon fresh lemon juice
- 3 packets unflavored gelatin
- 4 to 6 drops red or green liquid food coloring

1. Coat 8-inch-square baking pan with nonstick vegetable-oil cooking spray. Reserve $1/2$ cup applesauce. Mix remaining applesauce, ginger, $1^1/2$ cups sugar and salt in large skillet or Dutch oven. Bring to boiling; cook, uncovered, 25 minutes, stirring often to prevent sticking.

2. Stir lemon juice into reserved $1/2$ cup applesauce; stir in gelatin. Stir gelatin mixture and food coloring into applesauce mixture in skillet; cook 10 minutes more, stirring. Mixture will be very thick. Pour into prepared pan; spread level. Cool. Cut into 64 squares.

3. Place remaining $1/3$ cup sugar in small, shallow bowl; toss jellies in sugar to coat. Layer jellies between sheets of plastic wrap in airtight containers. Refrigerate for up to 1 month.

Yield: 64 jellies.

holiday cookie jar

$f$resh-baked cookies. Just the thought of them takes you back to childhood. Our old-fashioned **Christmas** collection features favorite flavors like **chocolate**, cherry and peppermint ... with a twist. Perfect for making new memories.

CHOCOLATE SANDWICH COOKIES

1¼ cups all-purpose flour
½ cup unsweetened cocoa powder
¾ teaspoon baking soda
¼ teaspoon salt
1 cup granulated sugar
½ cup (1 stick) unsalted butter, at room temperature
1 egg
½ teaspoon vanilla
¼ teaspoon mint extract

Filling:

2½ cups sifted confectioners' sugar
½ cup (1 stick) unsalted butter, at room temperature
2 tablespoons milk
½ teaspoon mint extract
Red and green food coloring

1. Sift together flour, cocoa, baking soda and salt into medium-size bowl; set aside. In large bowl, beat together sugar and butter until smooth and creamy. Beat in egg, then vanilla and mint extract.
2. On low speed of an electric mixer, beat flour mixture into butter mixture. Divide dough in half; shape each into a log about 1½ inches in diameter. Wrap in plastic wrap; refrigerate 3 to 4 hours.
3. Heat oven to 375°. Cut each log into slices, 3/16-inch thick; place on ungreased baking sheet.
4. Bake in 375° oven for 8 to 10 minutes or until almost firm. Transfer cookies to wire rack to cool.
5. Prepare Filling: Beat together confectioners' sugar, butter, milk and mint extract in medium-size bowl until mixture is a good spreading consistency. Divide filling in half; tint half with red food coloring and other half with green food coloring.
6. Spread flat side of one fourth of cookies with red filling and one fourth with green filling. Top each with a plain cookie. Chill until filling is set.
Yield: 3 dozen.

HOLIDAY WREATHS

You could actually use these as tree decorations if they weren't so tasty.

2¼ cups all-purpose flour
½ teaspoon baking powder
⅛ teaspoon salt
1 cup (2 sticks) unsalted butter, at room temperature
1½ cups confectioners' sugar
1 egg
1 teaspoon vanilla
Green soft gel paste food color
Red cinnamon candies

1. Heat oven to 400°.
2. Stir flour, baking powder and salt in medium-size bowl.
3. Beat butter and confectioners' sugar in bowl until smooth and creamy. Beat in egg and vanilla. At low speed of an electric mixer, beat flour mixture into butter mixture. Tint with green coloring. If dough is soft, refrigerate 30 minutes.
4. Place one fourth of dough in cookie gun fitted with small star disk. Press out a 5-inch line of dough onto ungreased baking sheet. Shape into wreath; place candies on top. Repeat with remaining dough and candies.
5. Bake in 400° oven for 6 to 8 minutes, until they just begin to brown. Transfer to wire rack to cool.
Yield: 4 dozen.

COCONUT-CHERRY MACAROONS

Coconut and almond are the palate-pleasers in these red-and-green-flecked morsels.

1 bag (7 ounces) sweetened flake coconut, coarsely chopped
½ cup canned almond filling
½ cup red glacé cherries, chopped
½ cup green glacé cherries, chopped
¼ cup sugar
¼ cup all-purpose flour
¼ teaspoon salt
2 egg whites, lightly beaten

1. Heat oven to 325°. Line large baking sheet with parchment paper.
2. Mix coconut, almond filling, cherries, sugar, flour, salt and egg whites in bowl.
3. Drop mixture by level tablespoonfuls onto prepared baking sheet; shape into balls.
4. Bake in 325° oven about 25 minutes, until lightly browned but still soft in center. Transfer to wire racks to cool.
Yield: About 2 dozen.

Delicious red and green mint filling peeks out from our Chocolate Sandwich Cookies (opposite). Red cinnamon candies make delectable holly berry accents on Holiday Wreaths (this page). Coconut-Cherry Macaroons (not pictured) boast an enticing almond taste.

VANILLA COOKIES

With simple additions and substitutions, you can make 12 more delicious varieties from the basic vanilla-flavored dough.

- 1$\frac{1}{4}$ cups all-purpose flour
- $\frac{1}{2}$ teaspoon baking powder
- $\frac{1}{4}$ teaspoon salt
- 3 tablespoons unsalted butter
- 3 tablespoons margarine
- $\frac{1}{2}$ cup sugar
- 1 egg
- $\frac{1}{2}$ teaspoon vanilla
- Vanilla Glaze (recipe follows)

1. Stir together flour, baking powder and salt in medium-size bowl.

2. Beat butter, margarine, sugar, egg and vanilla in bowl until well blended. Stir in flour mixture. Shape into ball; wrap in plastic wrap; refrigerate several hours or overnight.

3. Heat oven to 350°. Coat cookie sheet with nonstick vegetable-oil cooking spray.

4. Roll out dough on lightly floured surface to $\frac{3}{8}$-inch thickness. Cut into rounds with 2$\frac{1}{2}$-inch cookie cutter. Place on prepared baking sheets, spacing 1$\frac{1}{2}$ inches apart.

5. Bake in preheated 350° oven for 10 to 12 minutes or until lightly browned at edges. Transfer cookies to wire rack to cool. Frost with glaze, if you wish.
Yield: 2$\frac{1}{2}$ dozen.

Vanilla Glaze

Gradually stir 1 to 2 tablespoons milk or water into 1 cup confectioners' sugar until smooth and slightly runny. Add $\frac{1}{4}$ teaspoon vanilla. Tint with food coloring, if desired.

Orange Glaze

Omit vanilla and substitute orange juice for milk in Vanilla Glaze.

COOKIE DOUGH VARIATIONS

Refer to Vanilla Cookie recipe.

Coconut: Omit vanilla. Add $\frac{1}{2}$ teaspoon coconut extract to butter mixture; stir $\frac{1}{2}$ cup shredded coconut into flour mixture.

Nesselrode: Omit vanilla. Add $\frac{1}{2}$ teaspoon rum extract to butter mixture.

Coffee: Reduce vanilla to $\frac{1}{4}$ teaspoon. Dissolve 1 teaspoon instant coffee in 1 teaspoon very hot water; add to butter mixture. Add 1 teaspoon unsweetened cocoa powder to flour mixture.

Chocolate: Add 2 tablespoons unsweetened cocoa powder to flour mixture.

Orange: Omit vanilla. Add 1 teaspoon grated orange rind to butter mixture.

Hazelnut: Add $\frac{1}{2}$ cup finely chopped toasted hazelnuts to the flour mixture.

COOKIE SHAPES

Vanilla Trees: Cut out rolled Vanilla Cookie dough with 3$\frac{1}{2}$-inch tree cookie cutter. Bake as directed. Frost with green-tinted Vanilla Glaze when cool; decorate as desired with small candy "ornaments."

Coconut Thumbprints: Shape rounded measuring teaspoonfuls Coconut cookie dough into balls. Place on baking sheet. Roll balls in shredded coconut, place on baking sheet and place a chocolate candy in center. Bake as directed.

Nesselrode Drops: Drop rounded measuring teaspoonfuls Nesselrode cookie dough onto baking sheet. Press chopped mixed glacé fruits into tops of cookies. Bake as directed.

Coffee Wreaths: Cut chilled Coffee cookie dough into 16 equal pieces. Roll each piece on lightly floured surface into 20-inch rope. Cut in half. Fold each piece in half; twist loosely together. Shape each into a circle, pinching ends together. Place on baking sheet. Bake as directed. Brush with Vanilla Glaze when cool. Add gumdrop holly leaves and berry.

Choco-Orange Pinwheels: Roll half the Chocolate cookie dough into a 10 x 7-inch rectangle on lightly floured waxed paper. Repeat with half the Orange cookie dough. Place orange dough on top of chocolate dough so waxed paper is on top and bottom. Peel off top paper. Starting with a long side, roll up doughs tightly, jelly-roll fashion, using bottom waxed paper to lift dough. Wrap with waxed paper or plastic wrap and refrigerate until firm. Unwrap; cut into $\frac{1}{4}$-inch thick slices. Place on baking sheet. Bake as directed. Decorate with Orange Glaze, if desired.

Linzer Hazelnut Tarts: Cut out rolled Hazelnut cookie dough with a 2-inch round cookie cutter. With $\frac{3}{4}$-inch round cookie cutter, cut centers from half the circles. Place on baking sheet. Bake as directed. Sprinkle cut-out cookies with confectioners' sugar. When cool, sandwich 1 whole and 1 cut-out cookie together with raspberry preserves.

Simple Vanilla Cookies are the little black dress of desserts. With only a few alterations, they can be dressed up to suit any occasion!

Peppermint Wands (this page, from top), Coconut Snowballs and Chocolate Swirls are morsels even Santa will love. Fruity Sugar Plums (opposite) offer a delightful surprise tucked inside.

5. Bake in 350° oven for 8 to 10 minutes. Let stand for 2 minutes. Transfer cookies to wire rack to cool.

6. Decorate: Melt white chocolate chips and 1 teaspoon shortening in top of double boiler over hot water, stirring until smooth. Remove from heat but keep over hot water. Repeat with semisweet chocolate chips and 1 teaspoon shortening in top of second double boiler.

7. For drizzled lines, remove 2 tablespoons each of white and semisweet chocolate to 2 separate small bowls; place bowls in hot water. Add ¹/₂ teaspoon of shortening to each; stir to blend.

8. Dip half the cookies into white chocolate and other half into semisweet chocolate. Use spatula to spread chocolate evenly. Let excess chocolate drip off; set cookies on wire racks to dry.

9. When coating is dried, drizzle lines onto tops with contrasting color of chocolate. Let stand to set.

Yield: 9 dozen.

CHOCOLATE SWIRLS

There's chocolate everywhere in these cookies, inside and outside.

Cookies:

1	package (12 ounces) semisweet chocolate chips
2¹/₂	cups all-purpose flour
1	teaspoon baking soda
¹/₂	teaspoon salt
³/₄	cup (1¹/₂ sticks) butter or margarine, at room temperature
¹/₂	cup granulated sugar
¹/₂	cup firmly packed light-brown sugar
1	egg
2	egg whites
1	teaspoon vanilla

Decoration:

1¹/₂	cups white chocolate chips
3	teaspoons solid vegetable shortening
1¹/₄	cups semisweet chocolate chips

1. Heat oven to 350°.

2. Prepare Cookies: Melt chocolate in small saucepan over low heat, stirring occasionally until smooth.

3. Combine flour, baking soda and salt in a bowl.

4. Beat butter and sugars in bowl until creamy. Beat in egg, egg whites, melted chocolate and vanilla. At low speed of an electric mixer, gradually beat in flour mixture until combined. Drop dough by slightly rounded teaspoonfuls onto large ungreased baking sheet.

3. Bake in 350° oven for 10 to 12 minutes, until pale golden at edges. Transfer cookies to wire racks to cool.
4. Dip end of each cookie into chocolate; place on waxed-paper-lined baking sheets. Sprinkle dipped ends with candy. Refrigerate 20 minutes to set.
Yield: 7 dozen.

SUGAR PLUMS
A treat is hidden in each.

- 1/4 cup all-purpose flour
- 3/4 teaspoon salt
- 1/2 teaspoon baking powder
- 1/2 cup (1 stick) butter, at room temperature
- 1/2 cup sugar
- 1 egg
- 1 teaspoon vanilla
- 1/4 cup dark seedless raisins, finely chopped
- 1/4 cup pitted dates, finely chopped
- 1/4 cup pecans, finely chopped
- 1 tablespoon plum jam
  Colored decorator sugars
- 3 tablespoons butter, melted

1. Mix flour, salt and baking powder in medium-size bowl.
2. Beat together butter, sugar, egg and vanilla in small bowl until light and fluffy. Stir in flour mixture until well blended. Flatten dough into disk; wrap in plastic. Refrigerate until chilled, about 1 hour.
3. Combine raisins, dates, pecans and jam in a small bowl.
4. Break off rounded teaspoons of dough. With floured hands, roll into 3/4-inch balls. Make deep indentation in center of each ball. Spoon about 1/4 teaspoon raisin mixture into indentation in each center. Pinch dough closed, reshaping dough around raisin filling. Place on greased baking sheets. Refrigerate until chilled, about 1 hour.
5. Heat oven to 350°. Remove chilled dough from refrigerator.
6. Bake in 350° oven for 12 minutes. Transfer sugar plums to wire rack. Pour each color of decorator sugar into separate bowl. While cookies are still warm, brush with melted butter; roll cookies in sugar to coat. Cool on wire rack.
Yield: 3 dozen.

COCONUT SNOWBALLS
These yummy cookies are not made for throwing!

- 4 egg whites
- 1/4 teaspoon salt
- 2/3 cup sugar
- 1 teaspoon vanilla
- 1/4 cup all-purpose flour
- 3 cups sweetened flake coconut

1. Heat oven to 325°. Coat 2 baking sheets with nonstick vegetable-oil cooking spray.
2. Beat egg whites in bowl until stiff, glossy peaks form. Beat in salt, sugar, vanilla and flour. Stir in coconut. Drop batter by rounded teaspoonfuls, 1 inch apart, on prepared baking sheets.
3. Bake in 325° oven for 20 to 25 minutes, until lightly browned. Cool cookies briefly on sheets on wire rack. Transfer cookies to wire racks to cool.
Yield: 2 dozen.

PEPPERMINT WANDS
The taste magic comes from the candy-coated chocolate ends.

- 2 cups all-purpose flour
- 1/4 teaspoon salt
- 1 cup (2 sticks) unsalted butter, at room temperature
- 1 cup confectioners' sugar
- 2 teaspoons vanilla
- 12 ounces German sweet chocolate, melted
- 1/2 cup crushed red, green and white peppermint candies (about 20)

1. Line baking sheet with aluminum foil. Mix flour and salt. Beat butter and sugar in bowl until fluffy. Add vanilla. Beat in flour mixture. Cover and refrigerate dough 30 minutes.
2. Heat oven to 350°. Roll 1 teaspoon dough into 2 1/2-inch-long log. Place on prepared sheet. Repeat with remaining dough.

LIME SPRITZ WREATHS

1¼ cups all-purpose flour
¼ teaspoon salt
½ cup (1 stick) butter, at room temperature
⅓ cup granulated sugar
1 egg yolk
1 teaspoon very finely ground lime zest
½ teaspoon lemon extract
Green food color (optional)

Lime Frosting:
1 cup confectioners' sugar
1 tablespoon lime juice
Green food color (optional)
Water, as needed
Candy holly sprinkles, for decoration

1. Heat oven to 350°. Lightly grease large baking sheet.
2. Stir together flour and salt in a small bowl.
3. Beat together butter and sugar in medium-size bowl until creamy and smooth, about 2 minutes. Beat egg yolk into butter-sugar mixture. Add lime zest, lemon extract, and a few drops of green food color, if desired. Stir in flour mixture.
4. Press dough into cookie gun fitted with flower disk. Press dough onto ungreased baking sheet to make 32 cookies.
5. Bake in 350° oven for 10 to 12 minutes or until they just begin to brown. Transfer cookies to wire rack to cool.
6. Prepare Lime Frosting: Beat together 1 cup confectioners' sugar, 1 tablespoon lime juice and a drop or two of green food color, if desired, in small bowl. Add a little water, if needed to make good frosting consistency. Frost cookies. Decorate with candy holly sprinkles.
Yield: 32 cookies.

SPICE CUTOUTS

3 cups all-purpose flour
2 teaspoons ground cinnamon
2 teaspoons ground ginger
1 teaspoon ground cloves
¾ teaspoon salt
½ teaspoon ground nutmeg
½ teaspoon ground cardamom
1 cup (2 sticks) unsalted butter, at room temperature
1½ cups sugar
2 eggs
1 teaspoon vanilla
1 egg white mixed with 1 tablespoon water

1. Combine flour, cinnamon, ginger, cloves, salt, nutmeg and cardamom in bowl. Beat butter and sugar in large bowl until creamy. Beat in eggs and vanilla until fluffy. Stir in flour mixture. Divide dough in half; flatten into disks. Wrap in plastic. Refrigerate for 1 hour.
2. Heat oven to 350°. Coat 3½- to 4½-inch cookie-cutter molds with nonstick vegetable-oil cooking spray.
3. On lightly floured surface with floured rolling pin, roll out half of dough ¼-inch thick. Press cutter molds gently into dough. Gently pull cookies out of molds. Place on ungreased baking sheets. Brush with egg white; reroll scraps. Repeat with remaining dough.
4. Bake 10 to 12 minutes, until golden. Transfer to wire racks to cool. Store at room temperature or freeze.
Yield: 32 cookies.

STAINED-GLASS COOKIES

Hang as ornaments or wrap as a gift. It's your choice.

2³/4 cups all-purpose flour
¹/2 teaspoon baking powder
¹/2 teaspoon baking soda
¹/2 teaspoon salt
1 cup (2 sticks) unsalted butter, at room temperature
¹/2 cup sugar
¹/2 cup light corn syrup
¹/2 teaspoon almond extract
    Assorted hard candies

1. Heat oven to 350°. Line baking sheets with aluminum foil; lightly grease the foil.
2. Mix the flour, baking powder, baking soda and salt in bowl.
3. Beat butter and sugar in large bowl until light and fluffy. Beat in syrup and almond extract. At low speed of an electric mixer, beat in flour mixture. Divide dough in half; shape into disks. Wrap disks in plastic; refrigerate 20 minutes.

4. Sort candies by color. Pulverize each color separately in small food processor or blender with pulses, beginning with lightest color. Place different colors in separate small bowls. (If candy hardens, stir to loosen or reprocess in food processor or blender.)
5. Place one disk of dough between 2 sheets of waxed paper or plastic wrap. Roll out to ¹/4-inch thickness. Place on baking sheet. Remove top piece of paper. Using 3-inch holiday cookie cutters, cut dough into festive shapes. Using aspic cutters, tiny cookie cutters or paring knife, cut out shapes for the windowpanes. Place baking sheet with cookies in freezer for 10 minutes.
6. Remove from freezer. Lift dough from around cookies and inside windows. Remove cookies from waxed paper; place on foil-lined baking sheets. Reserve scraps.
7. Repeat with second disk of dough. Combine scraps to make more cookies.
8. Heat oven to 350°. Using the end of a vegetable peeler or very small spoon, fill cutout holes with pulverized candies; do not overflow edges. You may fill larger cutouts with several colors.

9. Bake in 350° oven for 8 to 10 minutes or until cookies are pale golden and candy just melts.
10. Remove sheets from oven. If desired, pierce top of cookies for hanging. For marbleized effect in multicolored windows, drag a wooden pick through candy before hardening. If dough has puffed up over cutout, use a small knife to gently pull back into shape while still warm. Transfer on foil to wire rack. When cool, gently peel away foil. Store cookies, layered between waxed paper, in airtight containers.
Yield: 2¹/2 dozen.

Use a kaleidoscope of colors in our scrumptious Stained-Glass Cookies (below). A welcome hint of citrus perks up Lime Spritz Wreaths (opposite, top). Sugar-cinnamon Spice Cutouts (opposite, bottom) get their zesty bite from ginger, cloves and nutmeg.

APPLE-RAISIN STICKY BUNS

Topping:

- ³/₄ cup firmly packed light-brown sugar
- 2 tablespoons butter, at room temperature
- ¹/₂ cup pecans, chopped

Buns:

- ¹/₄ cup firmly packed light-brown sugar
- 1 teaspoon ground cinnamon
- 1 pound frozen bread dough, thawed
- 1 tablespoon butter, melted
- ¹/₃ cup dark seedless raisins
- ¹/₂ cup pecans, chopped
- ¹/₃ cup chopped, peeled apple

1. Prepare Topping: Lightly coat 9-inch-round cake pan with nonstick vegetable-oil cooking spray.

2. Stir brown sugar and butter in small bowl to make paste. Spread over bottom of prepared pan; mixture may not cover bottom completely. Top with the pecans.

3. Prepare Buns: Mix brown sugar and cinnamon in small bowl.

4. On lightly floured surface, roll thawed bread dough out into 12 x 10-inch rectangle. Brush with melted butter. Sprinkle cinnamon mixture evenly over dough, leaving ¹/₂-inch border all around edge. Sprinkle raisins, pecans and apples evenly over the sugar mixture.

5. Starting from a long side, roll up dough, jelly-roll style. With serrated knife, cut roll crosswise into 9 equal pieces (you may want to trim ends of roll first). Place pieces, cut side down, in prepared pan. With cooking spray, coat piece of plastic wrap large enough to cover pan; place, coated side down, over rolls. Refrigerate to rise overnight.

6. Remove cake pan with buns from the refrigerator; let stand for 30 minutes.

7. Heat oven to 350°. Remove the plastic wrap.

8. Bake in 350° oven for 20 minutes or until golden. Cool buns in pan on wire rack for 5 minutes. Invert large serving platter over pan; carefully invert pan and platter. Remove pan, letting any sugar mixture in pan drip over buns. Serve warm or at room temperature.

Yield: 9 servings.

Visions of sugarplums? How about **sticky** buns? Our yummy breakfast recipes can be prepared ahead, so a little advance planning is all it takes to turn out **tasty** treats for some very merry munching come Christmas morn.

No one will be able to turn down warm mouth-watering, Apple-Raisin Sticky Buns. You'll have the whole family begging for more.

breakfast
goodies

BLUEBERRY CREAM CHEESE COFFEECAKE

Coffeecake:

2³/₄ cups all-purpose flour
1 cup firmly packed light-brown sugar
1 cup (2 sticks) unsalted butter, at room temperature
¹/₂ teaspoon baking powder
¹/₂ teaspoon baking soda
¹/₄ teaspoon salt
³/₄ cup sour cream
3 eggs
1 teaspoon almond extract
2 packages (8 ounces each) cream cheese, at room temperature
¹/₂ cup granulated sugar
1 teaspoon vanilla
¹/₂ cup fruit preserves
1 cup blueberries (if using frozen, drain and pat dry after thawing)
1 teaspoon ground cinnamon
¹/₂ cup chopped pistachio nuts

Glaze:

¹/₂ cup white chocolate chips
1 tablespoon solid vegetable shortening

1. Prepare Coffeecake: Heat oven to 350°. Grease and flour a 10-inch springform pan.

2. Pulse flour and brown sugar in processor twice to mix. Add butter; pulse until mixture resembles coarse meal, about 10 pulses. Remove 2 cups; reserve.

3. Add baking powder, baking soda, salt, sour cream, 1 egg and almond extract to mixture in processor. Process 30 seconds. With floured hands, spread dough over bottom and slightly up sides of prepared pan.

4. Beat cream cheese, granulated sugar, vanilla and remaining 2 eggs in bowl. Pour over crust. Carefully spoon preserves over cream cheese mixture. With knife, swirl preserves through mixture. Scatter blueberries over top.

5. Add cinnamon and nuts to reserved crumble mixture. Sprinkle on top of cake.

6. Bake in 350° oven 65 to 70 minutes, until almost set and top is golden brown. Place pan on rack; cool 15 minutes. Remove sides of pan. Cool.

Couple your day's first cup of java with a slice of ambrosial Blueberry Cream Cheese Coffeecake. Bake a day ahead for no hassle in the morn.

7. Prepare Glaze: Microwave white chocolate chips and shortening in microwave-safe bowl on full power 5 seconds. Stir. Microwave in 15-second increments, stirring after each increment, until chocolate is melted. Drizzle over cooled cake.

Yield: 12 to 16 servings.

HOLIDAY CRESCENT ROLL-UPS

- 1 cup golden seedless raisins
- 1 cup chopped hazelnuts
- ½ cup firmly packed light-brown sugar
- 1 teaspoon ground cinnamon
- 3 packages (8 ounces each) refrigerated crescent rolls
- ⅓ cup apricot preserves, warmed
  Confectioners' sugar (optional)

1. Heat oven to 375°. Lightly grease 2 baking sheets.
2. Mix together raisins, hazelnuts, brown sugar and cinnamon in large bowl.
3. On lightly floured surface, open and unroll crescent roll dough. Divide into triangles along perforations. Brush each triangle lightly with apricot preserves. Place 1 tablespoon of nut mixture in center of each triangle. Starting with short end, roll up each triangle. Place on prepared sheets.
4. Bake in 375° oven 10 to 13 minutes or until golden brown. Dust with confectioners' sugar, if desired.
Yield: 24 crescents.

POPPY SEED-LEMON SURPRISE MUFFINS

- 3 cups all-purpose flour
- 1 cup sugar
- 4 teaspoons baking powder
- 1 teaspoon salt
- 1½ tablespoons poppy seeds
- 2 eggs
- 1 cup milk
- ½ cup vegetable oil
- ¼ cup bottled lemon curd

1. Heat oven to 400°. Coat muffin pan with nonstick vegetable-oil cooking spray.
2. Mix flour, sugar, baking powder, salt and seeds in bowl.
3. In second bowl, mix eggs, milk and oil. Stir in flour mixture.
4. Fill muffin cups half full with batter. Place 1 teaspoon lemon curd in each cup. Top with batter.
5. Bake in 400° oven 20 to 25 minutes. Cool muffins on rack.
Yield: 12 muffins.
Make-Ahead Tip: Store muffins in an airtight container and freeze up to a month.

PUMPKIN-CRANBERRY SCONES

Scones:
- 2 cups all-purpose flour
- 2 tablespoons light-brown sugar
- 2 teaspoons pumpkin-pie spice
- 1 teaspoon baking powder
- ½ teaspoon grated orange zest
- ½ teaspoon salt
- ½ cup (1 stick) unsalted butter, cut into pieces and chilled
- ½ cup dried cranberries
- ½ cup chopped walnuts
- ½ cup canned solid-pack pumpkin purée (not pie filling)
- ½ cup heavy cream
- ½ teaspoon vanilla

Glaze:
- 1 egg yolk
- ¼ cup heavy cream
- 1 tablespoon sugar
- 1 teaspoon grated orange zest

1. Heat oven to 400°. Line large baking sheet with parchment paper.
2. Prepare Scones: Mix flour, brown sugar, spice, baking powder, zest and salt in bowl. Cut in butter until mixture resembles coarse meal. Add cranberries and nuts.
3. Mix pumpkin, cream and vanilla in bowl. Fold into flour mixture.
4. Turn dough out onto floured surface; knead 10 times. Pat into two 8-inch circles on prepared baking sheet. Cut each circle into 8 pie-shaped wedges.
5. Prepare Glaze: Mix yolk and cream. Brush over scones. Mix sugar and zest. Sprinkle over scones.
6. Bake in 400° oven for 16 minutes or until golden. Let cool.
Yield: 16 scones.

A snowy dusting of confectioners' sugar makes *Holiday Crescent Roll-Ups* (from top) an irresistible choice. For a bite that delights, try tangy *Poppy Seed-Lemon Surprise Muffins.* You'll also love tart and tasty *Pumpkin-Cranberry Scones,* which can be frozen ahead of time and brought out to thaw Christmas Eve. Sprinkle sugar and orange zest over the tops for a flavorful finish.

STOLLEN

- 1 envelope active dry yeast
- ³/₄ cup warm water (105° to 115°)
- ¹/₂ cup granulated sugar
- ¹/₂ teaspoon salt
- 3 eggs
- 1 egg yolk
- ¹/₂ cup (1 stick) butter, at room temperature
- 3¹/₂ cups all-purpose flour
- ¹/₂ cup chopped almonds
- ¹/₂ cup minced candied fruit
- ¹/₄ cup dark seedless raisins

Glaze:

- 1 cup sifted confectioners' sugar
- 1 tablespoon hot tap water
- ¹/₂ teaspoon vanilla
- ¹/₂ cup sliced almonds (optional)

1. Sprinkle yeast over the warm water in large bowl. Let stand until foamy, about 5 minutes. Stir to dissolve.

2. Add sugar, salt, eggs, yolk, butter and 1³/₄ cups flour to yeast. Beat at medium speed for 10 minutes. Add remaining flour, almonds, fruit and raisins. Cover; let rise in warm place 2 hours (dough will not double). Refrigerate overnight.

3. Turn dough out onto lightly floured surface. Divide in half. Shape each half into a 10 x 7-inch oval. Fold each oval in half lengthwise. Lightly grease large baking sheet. Place loaves on sheet. Cover; let rise in warm place 1¹/₂ hours or until doubled.

4. Heat oven to 375°. Bake for 20 minutes or until lightly golden. Transfer loaves to wire racks.

5. Prepare Glaze: Whisk confectioners' sugar, hot water and vanilla in small bowl. Pour over loaves. Sprinkle with nuts, if desired. Let cool.

Yield: 2 loaves.

Candied fruit and almonds make savory Stollen (above) an a.m. delight. Breakfast Potpie (opposite, top) is a robust redux of run-of-the-mill sausage and eggs. Serve up a heaping helping to revelers with hearty appetites. You'll go nuts for Overnight Cappuccino French Toast With Pecan Pralines and our Pear-Cherry Dutch-Style Pancake (opposite, bottom). Their sophistication is matched only by their simplicity.

BREAKFAST POTPIE

1 pound country-style breakfast
    sausage
1 large shallot, minced
1/2 pound fresh mushrooms, sliced
1 package (8 ounces) cream cheese,
    cut into chunks
8 eggs
1/4 cup packaged, unseasoned bread
    crumbs
1 frozen puff pastry sheet, thawed
    following package directions
2 tablespoons butter, melted

1. Brown sausage in skillet, about
5 minutes. Set sausage aside. Add shallot
to skillet; sauté until softened, about
2 minutes. Add mushrooms; sauté until
browned, about 6 minutes. Add cream
cheese and sausage to skillet; cook,
stirring, until cheese has melted, about
3 minutes. Spoon sausage mixture into
an 8 x 8 x 2-inch baking pan.
2. In same skillet, scramble eggs, leaving
slightly undercooked. Spoon eggs over
sausage. Sprinkle with crumbs.
3. On floured surface, roll pastry to a
9-inch square. Brush with some melted
butter. Place on baking pan, butter side
down; crimp edges. Brush with butter.
Cut 5 steam vents. (Pie can be
refrigerated overnight or frozen up to
1 month. Increase baking time for frozen
potpie by 15 minutes.)
4. To bake, heat oven to 350°. Bake
about 30 minutes or until pastry is
golden brown and filling is bubbly.
Yield: 6 servings.

OVERNIGHT CAPPUCCINO FRENCH TOAST WITH PECAN PRALINES

Toast:

1 loaf (16 ounces) French bread
8 eggs
2 cups half-and-half
1 cup milk
1 teaspoon vanilla
2 tablespoons granulated sugar
1 1/2 teaspoons instant espresso
    powder
1/4 teaspoon ground cinnamon
1/8 teaspoon ground nutmeg
1/4 teaspoon salt

Praline Topping:

1 cup (2 sticks) butter
1 cup firmly packed light-brown
    sugar
2 tablespoons light corn syrup
1/2 teaspoon ground cinnamon
1/2 cup chopped pecans

1. Prepare Toast: Coat 13 x 9 x 2-inch
baking pan with nonstick vegetable-oil
cooking spray.
2. Slice bread into 1-inch-thick slices.
Arrange in prepared pan.
3. Whisk eggs, half-and-half, milk,
vanilla, sugar, espresso powder,
cinnamon, nutmeg and salt in bowl.
Pour over bread. Cover; refrigerate
overnight.
4. Next morning, heat oven to 400°.
5. Prepare Topping: In small saucepan,
heat butter, brown sugar, syrup and
cinnamon over medium heat, stirring
occasionally, until smooth, 5 to
7 minutes. Add pecans. Remove
from heat.
6. Remove pan from refrigerator.
Uncover; pour on toppng.
7. Bake in 400° oven for 40 minutes
or until heated through.
Yield: 6 servings.

PEAR-CHERRY DUTCH-STYLE PANCAKE

Fruit:

1/4 cup firmly packed light-brown
    sugar
1/4 teaspoon ground cinnamon
2 medium-size pears, peeled, cored
    and thickly sliced
1/4 cup dried tart cherries
1 tablespoon water
1 tablespoon cherry-flavored
    liqueur (optional)

Pancake:

1/3 cup water
2 tablespoons unsalted butter
1/4 cup biscuit mix
2 eggs

1. Prepare Fruit: Mix brown sugar and
cinnamon in bowl. Add pears. Cover
and refrigerate.
2. Mix cherries, water and liqueur,
if using, in bowl. Let stand 20 to
30 minutes.
3. Heat oven to 400°.
4. Prepare Pancake: Bring 1/3 cup water
and butter to boiling in saucepan.
Reduce to low. Add baking mix; stir
vigorously to form a ball. Remove from
heat. Beat in eggs, one at a time. Beat
until batter is smooth, about 2 minutes.
Spread in ungreased 9-inch pie plate.
Drain pears; spread on pancake, leaving
1-inch border. Drain cherries; sprinkle
on top.
5. Bake in 400° oven 20 to 25 minutes
or until edges are puffed and golden
brown. Serve.
Yield: 6 servings.
Make-Ahead Tip: Pear and cherry
mixture can be made up to a day ahead.
Prepare batter just before baking.

meringue magic

What is it about meringue that is so thoroughly **beguiling**? Could it be its ethereal nature, the light-as-a-cloud consistency? Perhaps it's the way that you can sculpt it into myriad **whimsical** forms. Or is it much **simpler** than all that? Maybe it's merely the melt-in-your-mouth goodness.

Meringue Snowmen and Christmas Trees could make even Scrooge chuckle, and they're a breeze to assemble. We decked ours out with colored sugar, nonpareils, sugar stars and cinnamon drops.

MERINGUE SNOWMEN

3 egg whites, at room temperature
¾ cup sugar (see Note, page 85)
½ teaspoon cream of tartar
¼ teaspoon salt
½ teaspoon lemon or orange extract
    Royal Icing (recipe, page 87)
    Small red and green star-shaped
        sugar candies and red
        cinnamon
    Assorted soft gel food colors

1. Position racks in second and third levels in oven. Heat oven to 200°. Line 2 baking sheets with parchment paper or aluminum foil.

2. Beat egg whites, 2 tablespoons sugar, cream of tartar and salt at medium speed in small bowl until frothy. Increase speed to high; beat until soft peaks form. Gradually beat in remaining sugar, 1 tablespoon at a time, until stiff and glossy peaks form, about 5 minutes. Beat in extract.

3. If using parchment paper, place dab of meringue under each corner to keep paper from curling. Transfer meringue into large pastry bag fitted with coupler. Pipe twenty-four 1½-inch balls on prepared baking sheet. With slightly wet fingertip, smooth meringue to shape into ball, if necessary. Affix a #12 large round tip to coupler; pipe twenty-four 1-inch balls (see photo 1, this page). Remove #12 tip, and replace with a #10 medium round tip. Pipe 24 heads for snowmen.

4. Bake meringues in 200° oven 1¼ hours or until firm and dry; turn and reverse sheets halfway through. Turn oven off; let sit in closed oven 1 hour.

5. Remove baking sheets to wire rack to cool 10 minutes. Carefully lift off meringues.

6. Prepare Royal Icing.

7. Assemble snowmen, using the icing as glue (see photo 2): Beginning with a large ball as base, attach a body and a head with dabs of icing. Repeat with remaining bases, bodies and heads.

8. Decorate as desired, using icing to attach candy "buttons." Tint small amount of icing orange, and small amount black. Use toothpick to fashion eyes, mouths and "carrot" noses.

9. Serve or store in airtight container at room temperature for up to 1 week.
Yield: 2 dozen snowmen.

MERINGUE CHRISTMAS TREES

3 egg whites, at room temperature
¾ cup sugar (see Note, page 85)
½ teaspoon cream of tartar
¼ teaspoon salt
½ teaspoon peppermint extract
    Green soft gel paste food color
    White-, red- and green-colored
        nonpareils
    Rainbow-colored sprinkles
    Royal Icing (recipe, page 87)

1. Position oven racks in second and third levels in oven. Heat oven to 200°. Line 2 large baking sheets with parchment paper or aluminum foil. Fit large pastry bag with large star tip.

2. Beat egg whites, 2 tablespoons sugar, cream of tartar and salt at medium speed in small bowl until frothy. Increase speed to high; beat until soft peaks form. Gradually beat in remaining sugar, 1 tablespoon at a time, until stiff and glossy peaks form, about 5 minutes. Add peppermint extract and tint with green food color, beating until blended.

3. If using parchment paper, place dab of meringue under each corner to keep paper from curling. Spoon meringue into pastry bag with large star tip. Pipe meringue into thirty 2-inch stars, spacing about 1 inch apart, onto prepared baking sheet. Using slightly less pressure on pastry bag, pipe thirty 1-inch stars (see photo 3, this page) onto baking sheet. Using even less pressure on pastry bag, pipe thirty ¾-inch stars onto baking sheet.

4. Decorate meringue stars, sprinkling with nonpareils and sprinkles.

5. Bake meringues in 200° oven for 2 hours or until firm and dry, turning and reversing baking sheets halfway through baking. Remove the baking sheets to wire racks to cool for 10 minutes. Carefully transfer stars from baking sheets to wire racks to cool completely. (If baking on aluminum foil, it may be necessary to gently loosen meringue stars with a thin metal spatula to remove).

6. Prepare Royal Icing.

7. For each tree, stack 3 meringue stars of graduated size on top of each other, securing stars together with Royal Icing. Serve meringue trees immediately or store in airtight container at room temperature for up to 1 week.
Yield: 2½ dozen trees.

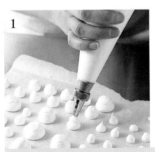

SNOWMEN: (photo 1) To form, fit large pastry bag with a coupler; fill bag with meringue. Without connecting a tip, pipe twenty-four 1½-inch balls for bases. Affix a #12 large round tip to coupler. Pipe about 24 middles. Change to a #10 medium round tip, and pipe 24 heads. Bake as directed in recipe. Once the meringue snowballs have baked and are dry to the touch, prepare Royal Icing (page 87). Carefully remove snowballs from parchment paper. Begin with a large snowball for the base. Using Royal Icing like glue, attach a middle and a top snowball to make the snowman body and head (photo 2). If the meringue is at all sticky, coat your hands with a small amount of cornstarch. To keep meringues from getting tacky, store in airtight containers. Meringues may be recrisped in 200° oven for 10 to 15 minutes.

CHRISTMAS TREES: To make trees, scrape green tinted meringue into large pastry bag fitted with a large star tip. Pipe graduated stars by varying the pressure applied to pastry bag (photo 3).

Playful Mocha Meringue Kisses are guaranteed to delight. Tuck them inside Basketweave Boxes for a romantic touch.

MOCHA MERINGUE KISSES

- 3 egg whites, at room temperature
- 1/2 teaspoon cream of tartar
- 1/4 teaspoon salt
- 3/4 cup sugar (see Note, this page)
- 1/2 teaspoon vanilla
- 2 tablespoons unsweetened cocoa powder
- 1 tablespoon espresso powder

Dipping Chocolate:
- 1 cup semisweet chocolate chips

1. Position oven racks in second and third levels of oven. Heat oven to 200°. Fit large pastry bag with a 1/2-inch star tip. Line 2 large baking sheets with parchment paper or aluminum foil.

2. Beat together egg whites, cream of tartar and salt at medium speed in small bowl until foamy. Gradually add sugar, 1 tablespoon at a time, beating until stiff and glossy peaks form, about 5 minutes. Beat in vanilla. Fold in cocoa powder and espresso powder until well blended.

3. If using parchment paper, dab a small amount of meringue under each corner to keep paper from curling.

4. Spoon meringue into pastry bag fitted with star tip. Pipe 1 1/2-inch kisses about 1 inch apart onto prepared baking sheets.

5. Bake in 250° oven for 1 1/4 to 1 1/2 hours or until meringues give slightly when gently pressed and are dry to touch; turn and reverse position of sheets halfway through baking. Turn oven off. Let meringues sit in closed oven for 1 hour. Transfer meringues from parchment paper or foil to wire rack. (If using foil, it may be necessary to gently loosen with long, thin metal spatula before removing.)

6. Prepare Dipping Chocolate: Heat chocolate chips in small heavy saucepan over medium-low heat until melted and smooth. Cool slightly. Dip bottoms of meringue kisses in melted chocolate, allowing excess chocolate to drip back into saucepan. Transfer meringue kisses to waxed-paper-lined baking sheets; let cool until chocolate hardens. Serve immediately or store in airtight container.

Yield: 5 dozen kisses.

BASKETWEAVE BOXES

- 3 egg whites, at room temperature
- 1/2 teaspoon cream of tartar
- 1/4 teaspoon salt
- 3/4 cup sugar (see Note, this page)
- 1/2 teaspoon almond extract
  Royal Icing (recipe, page 87)

1. Position racks in second and third levels in oven. Heat oven to 200°. Fit large pastry bag with a medium basketweave tip.

2. Line 2 large baking sheets with parchment paper or aluminum foil. Trace thirty 2-inch squares, about 1/2 inch apart. (If using parchment, flip paper over after tracing because markings may come off onto meringue).

3. Beat egg whites, cream of tartar and salt at medium speed in small bowl until foamy. Gradually add sugar, 1 tablespoon at a time, beating until stiff and glossy peaks form, about 5 minutes. Beat in extract.

4. Spoon meringue into pastry bag. Pipe 6 bottoms for the boxes, over 6 squares (these don't need to be neat, because they will be hidden). Pipe remaining meringue into 2-inch basketweave squares: Pipe straight line along edge of one square. Across meringue line, pipe 4 short stripes, about 3/4 inch long, spacing stripes apart the width of basketweave tip. Pipe second straight line, parallel to first, and overlapping short stripes. Pipe next set of cross-lines in spaces between first set of cross-stripes and overlapping the second line. Continue alternating short stripes with solid lines (photo, this page), until square is covered. Repeat "weaving" remaining squares.

5. Bake meringues in 200° oven for 2 hours or until firm and dry, turning and reversing baking sheets halfway through baking.

6. Remove baking sheets to wire rack to cool 10 minutes, or until cool to the touch. Very gently loosen meringues with thin metal spatula; transfer squares to wire racks.

7. Prepare Royal Icing. Fit pastry bag with #10 round writing tip. Holding 2 edges of 2 squares together at right angle, pipe icing along seam (may be necessary to trim squares with thin serrated knife to even edges). Repeat with 2 more squares; attach to first 2 to make 4-sided box. Pipe icing on top outside edges of one of 6 box bottoms. Set 4-sided box on bottom. Place on parchment paper or aluminum foil to dry. Repeat for 5 more boxes.

8. Serve immediately or store in airtight containers for up to 1 week.

Yield: 6 boxes.

Note: For a smoother textured meringue mixture, whirl the sugar in a blender or food processor for 2 minutes or until the sugar is finely ground, scraping down the sides as needed. You may also substitute super-fine sugar for granulated sugar.

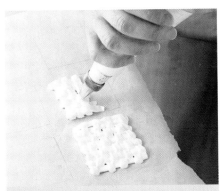

A TISKET, A TASKET: To make a basketweave square, first draw 2-inch squares onto parchment paper. Invert traced side of paper onto baking sheet or tracing may come off onto meringue during baking. Spoon meringue into large pastry bag fitted with a medium-size basketweave tip. Pipe a straight line following edge of square. Pipe 4 short stripes from same edge, starting on top of line; space stripes about 1/2 inch apart, or the width of the basketweave tip. Make another vertical line, parallel to first, overlapping short stripes. Pipe out next set of horizontals by burying tip under first vertical.

CRANBERRY-ORANGE CREAM-FILLED MERINGUE TORTE

  6 egg whites, at room temperature
 3/4 teaspoon cream of tartar
 1/4 teaspoon salt
 1 1/2 cups sugar (see Note, page 85)
  1 teaspoon orange extract

Cranberry Topping:

 1 1/2 cups sugar
 2/3 cup water
  3 cups fresh cranberries
  2 teaspoons grated orange zest
 1/4 teaspoon salt

Cranberry Chantilly:

 1 1/2 cups heavy cream
  2 tablespoons confectioners' sugar
  1 teaspoon orange extract

Thin slices orange, for garnish

1. Prepare Meringue: Position oven racks in second and third levels in oven. Heat oven to 250°. Trace three 8-inch circles on parchment-lined or aluminum foil-lined baking sheets. (If using parchment, flip paper over after tracing because markings may come off on meringue.). Fit large pastry bag with large star decorating tip.
2. Beat whites, cream of tartar and salt at medium speed in bowl until soft peaks form. Gradually add sugar, 1 tablespoon at a time, beating until stiff and glossy peaks form, about 5 minutes. Beat in extract.
3. If using parchment paper, place dab of meringue under each corner to prevent curling. Fill pastry bag with one third of meringue. Starting at just inside of one traced circle, pipe a decorative edge around entire circle. Starting in center, pipe meringue in a spiral to fill in circle. Repeat with remaining meringue and circles.
4. Bake in 250° oven for 1 hour or until tops are dry and smooth and yield slightly when pressed with fingertip, turning and reversing baking sheets halfway through baking. Turn oven off. Let meringue stand in closed oven 1 hour or overnight.
5. Remove baking sheets to wire rack to cool 10 minutes. Remove meringue from parchment or foil to wire rack to completely cool. (If baking on foil, it may be necessary to gently loosen foil from meringue with long, thin metal spatula before removing).
6. Meanwhile, prepare Cranberry Topping: Stir sugar and water in saucepan to dissolve sugar. Bring to boiling over medium heat; cook 5 minutes. Add cranberries; gently boil until skins start to pop, for 5 to 8 minutes. Stir in orange zest and salt. Pour into small heat-proof bowl; refrigerate 1 hour.
7. Prepare Cranberry Chantilly: Beat cream, confectioners' sugar and orange extract in medium-size bowl until soft peaks form; fold in 3/4 cup cranberry topping.
8. Place 1 meringue circle on serving platter. Spoon half of chantilly over top. Top with second meringue. Spoon on remaining chantilly. Place third meringue on top. Cover with Cranberry topping. Garnish with orange slices. Serve immediately or let stand for 1 hour to soften meringue slightly.
Yield: 10 servings.

MERINGUE POINSETTIAS

- 3 egg whites, at room temperature
- 1/2 teaspoon cream of tartar
- 1/4 teaspoon salt
- 3/4 cup sugar (see Note, page 85)
- 1 teaspoon vanilla

  Red and yellow soft gel paste food colors

  Red decorator sugar (optional)

  Royal Icing (recipe follows)

1. Position oven racks in second and third levels in oven. Heat oven to 200°. Fit large pastry bag with small flat or medium round decorating tip. Fit small pastry bag with writing tip. Line 2 large baking sheets with parchment paper or aluminum foil. Trace poinsettia pattern (page 136) onto sheets, using 5 petals per flower and spacing flowers about 1 inch apart. (If using parchment, flip paper over after tracing because markings may come off on meringue.)

2. Beat egg whites, cream of tartar and salt at medium speed in small bowl until foamy. Add sugar, 1 tablespoon at a time, beating until stiff, glossy peaks form, about 5 minutes. Beat in vanilla. Tint meringue light pink using red food color.

3. Spoon pink meringue into large pastry bag. Working with flat side of tip facing up, outline petals with meringue, wiping tip after each piping. Fill in each petal with meringue. Sprinkle generously with red sugar, if desired.

Pick a petal off our Meringue Poinsettias. Their dainty beauty is incomparable, their sugar flavor sublime. The Cranberry-Orange Cream-Filled Meringue Torte (opposite) is a taste of paradise.

4. Bake in 200° oven 1 1/4 to 1 1/2 hours or until meringues give slightly when gently pressed and are dry to the touch; turning and reversing position of sheets halfway through baking. Turn oven off. Let meringues sit in closed oven for 1 hour. Gently loosen poinsettias with long thin metal spatula. Carefully transfer meringues to wire rack to cool.

5. Prepare Royal Icing. Tint 1/2 cup Royal Icing yellow. Pipe 7 yellow dots in center of each meringue. Let stand until hardened. Serve immediately or store in airtight container for up to 1 week.

Yield: 22 poinsettias.

Royal Icing: In bowl, mix 1 pound confectioners' sugar, 3 tablespoons egg-white powder and 6 tablespoons water. Beat with an electric mixer on high speed 10 minutes, until thick and piping consistency.

Dinner Is Served

CREOLE SHRIMP DIP

To speed up prep, use pre-cooked shrimp from your local fish store or supermarket.

- 1 pound medium-size shrimp, shelled and deveined
- 1 clove garlic, minced
- 1/4 teaspoon chopped fresh thyme
- 1 tablespoon olive oil
- 1/2 pound 1/3-less-fat cream cheese, at room temperature
- 1/3 cup finely diced sweet red pepper
- 1/3 cup finely diced sweet green pepper
- 2 scallions, minced
- 1 tablespoon fresh lemon juice
- 1/2 teaspoon Worcestershire sauce
- 1/2 teaspoon hot-pepper sauce
- 3/4 teaspoon salt
- 1/4 teaspoon ground black pepper
- 1/2 cup sour cream
  Rice crackers and fresh vegetables, such as snow peas, carrots, sweet red pepper, broccoli and cauliflower flowerets, for serving

1. Simmer shrimp and 3 cups water in saucepan until shrimp are opaque in thickest part, about 10 minutes. Drain in colander; rinse under cold water. Reserve 1 or 2 shrimp for garnish; finely chop remainder.

2. Sauté garlic and thyme in oil in small skillet over low heat until garlic is softened but not browned, about 3 to 5 minutes.

3. Mix cream cheese and garlic mixture in large bowl. Stir in all but 1 teaspoon red and green peppers, scallions, lemon juice, Worcestershire, pepper sauce, salt and pepper. Stir in chopped shrimp and sour cream. Cover and chill.

4. Stir dip. Adjust salt and pepper sauce, if desired. Mound dip in serving dish. Garnish with reserved whole shrimp and remaining chopped peppers. Surround with crackers and vegetables for dipping. **Yield:** About 3 cups.

Capture the flavor and fun of New Orleans with zesty Creole Shrimp Dip. Accompany with handy scoopers such as rice crackers, snow peas, carrots and red peppers.

Carrot-Pear Soup and Onion-Topped Biscuits are a nice beginning — and easy, too.

ONION-TOPPED BISCUITS

Onion Topping:
- 1 tablespoon butter
- 1 Spanish onion, thinly sliced (about ¹/₂ pound)
- ³/₄ teaspoon dried leaf rosemary, crumbled
- ¹/₄ teaspoon salt

Biscuit Dough:
- 2 cups all-purpose flour
- 1 tablespoon baking powder
- ¹/₂ teaspoon dried leaf rosemary, crumbled
- ¹/₂ teaspoon salt
- ¹/₃ cup vegetable shortening
- ³/₄ cup buttermilk

1. Prepare Onion Topping: Heat butter in medium-size skillet over low heat. Add onion, rosemary and salt; sauté until softened, about 15 minutes. Remove from heat.

2. Heat oven to 450°.

3. Prepare Biscuit Dough: Sift together flour, baking powder, rosemary and salt into a bowl.

4. Using 2 knives or pastry blender, cut shortening into flour mixture until it resembles coarse meal. Make a well in center of dry ingredients. Pour in buttermilk all at once. Stir quickly with fork to form dough.

5. Turn dough out onto floured board. Gently knead 2 or 3 times. Pat dough into ³/₄-inch-thick piece. Cut out biscuits with floured 2-inch biscuit cutter. Place on ungreased baking sheet. Press scraps together (do not knead). Cut out more biscuits. Top each biscuit with onion topping.

6. Bake in 450° oven 12 to 14 minutes or until lightly browned. Cool biscuits on baking sheet on wire rack for 2 to 3 minutes. Serve immediately.

Yield: 8 biscuits.

Welcome family and friends **home** for the holidays with a **bountiful** feast of goodwill and good food. Old-fashioned fare with a few variations is guaranteed to please. So come one, come all to a merry celebration!

CARROT-PEAR SOUP

- 1 tablespoon butter
- 1 large onion, diced
- 2 cloves garlic, finely chopped
- 1 stalk celery, sliced
- 6 carrots, peeled and sliced
- 1 medium-size potato, peeled and cut in 1-inch pieces
- 2 pears, peeled, cored and cut in 1-inch pieces
- 1 bay leaf, broken in half
- 3 cans (13³/₄ ounces each) chicken broth
- ¹/₈ teaspoon ground black pepper
- 1 cup heavy cream, for garnish
  Chives, for garnish (optional)

1. Melt butter in large pot. Add onion, garlic and celery; sauté until softened, about 10 minutes. Add carrots, potato, pears, bay leaf and chicken broth. Cover; bring to boiling. Lower heat; simmer 40 minutes.

2. Remove bay leaf. Working in batches, pulse soup mixture in food processor or blender until smooth purée. Season with pepper.

3. Beat cream in a small bowl until stiff peaks form. Garnish each serving of soup with whipped cream. Garnish with chives, if you wish.

Yield: 8 servings (6 cups).

ROAST TURKEY BREAST WITH CORNBREAD-SAUSAGE STUFFING

- 1 whole turkey breast on bone (5½ to 6 pounds)
- ½ teaspoon salt
- ¼ teaspoon ground black pepper

Stuffing:

- 2 cups fresh or frozen (thawed) cranberries
- 1 cup water
- ½ cup sugar
- 1 pound Italian-style turkey sausage links, casings removed
- 7 to 8 cups crumbled cornbread (see Note)
- 1 large onion, chopped (about 1 cup)
- ½ cup chopped pecans
- ¼ cup chopped fresh parsley
- 1 tablespoon grated orange zest
- 1 teaspoon salt
- ½ teaspoon ground black pepper
- 1 cup reduced-sodium chicken broth

1. Rinse turkey breast and pat dry. Season cavity with salt and pepper. Place rack in roasting pan. Place aluminum foil on rack. Pierce foil in 6 places for excess liquid to drain. Place breast on foil, breast-side up.

2. Prepare Stuffing: Combine cranberries, water and sugar in medium-size saucepan. Bring to boiling over medium heat. Reduce heat to low; simmer 10 minutes. Drain well; transfer to large bowl.

3. Meanwhile, coat medium-size skillet with nonstick vegetable-oil cooking spray. Add sausage; sauté, breaking into large chunks with wooden spoon, until lightly browned, about 5 minutes. Drain excess fat. Add sausage to cranberries.

4. Add the cornbread, onion, pecans, parsley, orange zest, ½ teaspoon salt and ¼ teaspoon pepper to cranberry mixture. Pour chicken broth over cranberry mixture; toss until well combined.

5. Heat oven to 375°. Spoon about half of stuffing under breast and into cavity. Season outside of breast with remaining ½ teaspoon salt and ¼ teaspoon pepper.

Cover pan with lid or tight-fitting aluminum foil. Spoon remaining stuffing into greased 8 x 8 x 2-inch baking dish; cover with aluminum foil. Place in refrigerator.

6. Roast turkey in 375°oven for 1½ hours. Uncover; roast another 1 hour or until instant-read thermometer inserted into meat and into stuffing registers 165°. Place remaining dish of stuffing in oven for last 30 minutes of

baking. (For a crispy top, uncover stuffing for the last 10 minutes of baking.) Let turkey stand at least 20 minutes before carving. Serve with stuffing.

Yield: 12 servings.

Note: Make cornbread using the following recipe, your favorite recipe, or a 12-ounce box of corn muffin mix prepared according to package directions.

CORNBREAD

1 cup yellow cornmeal
1 cup all-purpose flour
1 tablespoon sugar
2 teaspoons baking powder
$1/2$ teaspoon salt
$1^1/4$ cups milk
$1/4$ cup ($1/2$ stick) butter, melted

1. Heat oven to 425°. Grease a 9-inch square baking pan.
2. Stir together cornmeal, flour, sugar, baking powder and salt in medium-size bowl. Stir in milk and melted butter just until dry ingredients are moistened. Pour batter into prepared pan.
3. Bake in 425° oven 20 to 25 minutes until center springs back when lightly touched. Cool.
Yield: 9 servings (7 to 8 cups crumbled for stuffing).

GREEN BEANS WITH RED PEPPER STRIPS

$1^1/2$ pounds fresh green beans
2 sweet red peppers, cut into $1/4$-inch strips
$1/4$ cup sliced green onions
2 teaspoons grated lemon zest
2 tablespoons lemon juice
2 tablespoons olive oil
$1/2$ teaspoon salt
$1/8$ teaspoon ground black pepper

1. Cook beans in large pot of lightly salted boiling water 12 to 15 minutes or until tender. Add pepper strips and green onions; cook 2 minutes. Drain; place in serving bowl.
2. Meanwhile, whisk together lemon zest, lemon juice, olive oil, salt and black pepper in small bowl.
3. Toss vegetables with lemon dressing. Serve immediately.
Yield: 8 servings.

SWEET POTATOES WITH PEACHES AND PECANS
This casserole can be made a day ahead.

$2^1/2$ pounds sweet potatoes (about 4), peeled and sliced $1/2$-inch thick (See Note)
1 can (16 ounces) peach halves, in light syrup
2 tablespoons butter
3 tablespoons rum
$1/2$ cup firmly packed light-brown sugar
1 teaspoon salt
$1/4$ teaspoon ground allspice
$1/8$ teaspoon ground nutmeg
$1/2$ cup pecan halves OR $1/4$ cup chopped pecans

1. Cook potato slices in large saucepan of boiling water until tender, 25 to 30 minutes. Drain.
2. Lightly grease a 13 x 9 x 2-inch baking dish. Drain peaches, reserving syrup.
3. Melt butter in saucepan. Add rum, reserved peach syrup, brown sugar, salt, allspice and nutmeg. Simmer 5 minutes. Cool.
4. Arrange sweet potato slices and peaches in prepared baking dish. Sprinkle with pecans. Pour sugar-rum mixture over top. Cover and refrigerate until ready to bake.
5. Bake in preheated 350° oven 25 to 30 minutes. Baste sweet potatoes and peaches with sugar-rum sauce from bottom of pan before serving.
Note: You may substitute two 24-ounce cans of yams, drained, for sweet potatoes. When making rum mixture, use only half the peach syrup and half the brown sugar. Reduce baking time to 20 minutes.
Yield: 8 servings.

CRANBERRY RELISH
This is best when made a day ahead.

3 cups cranberries (12-ounce bag)
1 cup apple juice
1 cup sugar
$1/4$ teaspoon ground allspice
1 large apple, cored and chopped

1. Combine cranberries, apple juice, sugar and allspice in medium-size non-reactive saucepan. Bring to boiling. Lower heat; simmer, uncovered, for 5 minutes.
2. Add chopped apple. Cook 5 minutes longer. Serve warm or chilled.
Yield: 12 servings.

GARLIC MASHED POTATOES
These potatoes can be made one day in advance.

3 pounds baking potatoes (about 6), peeled and cut in 2-inch chunks
$1/4$ cup ($1/2$ stick) unsalted butter
1 small onion, chopped
4 medium-size cloves garlic, sliced
$1/4$ cup potato-cooking water
1 cup milk
1 teaspoon salt

1. Place potatoes in large pot of cold water. Bring water to boiling; boil for 20 to 25 minutes or until tender.
2. Meanwhile, melt butter in small skillet over medium-low heat. Add onion and garlic; sauté until softened, about 15 minutes. Transfer onion mixture to a blender. Add the potato cooking water. Whirl until onion mixture forms a smooth paste. Set aside until ready to use.
3. Drain potatoes in colander; place in large bowl. Mash potatoes, using hand masher or electric mixer. Add milk, onion purée and salt. Beat until smooth. Serve immediately or transfer to $1^1/2$-quart microwave-safe serving dish. Cover with plastic wrap. Refrigerate until ready to reheat.
4. To reheat potatoes in microwave oven: Vent wrap at one corner of dish. Microwave on full power for 5 minutes or until heated through, stirring after 3 minutes.
Yield: 8 servings.

F*or smaller crowds, try a Roast Turkey Breast tempered with savory Cornbread-Sausage Stuffing (opposite). Perfect turkey go-withs include flavorful Cranberry Relish, lemony Green Beans with Red Pepper Strips and Sweet Potatoes with Peaches and Pecans. Garlic Mashed Potatoes (not pictured) are a tried-and-true favorite worthy of Mama's kitchen.*

Creamy Pumpkin Caramel Flan (below) is a luscious alternative to pumpkin pie. Maple-Pear Tart Tatin (opposite, from top), Streusel-Topped Apple-Sour Cream Pie and seasonal fruit offer a refreshing finale for your family feast.

STREUSEL-TOPPED APPLE-SOUR CREAM PIE

- 2 tablespoons unsalted butter
- 3 pounds baking apples, such as Granny Smith, peeled, cored and sliced into eighths
- 1 cup granulated sugar
- 1 teaspoon vanilla
- 1 cup chopped walnuts
- $3/4$ cup firmly packed dark-brown sugar
- $3/4$ cup all-purpose flour
- 1 teaspoon ground cinnamon
- $1/4$ teaspoon salt
- 6 tablespoons unsalted butter, cut into pieces and chilled
- $3/4$ cup sour cream
- $1/8$ teaspoon grated nutmeg
- 1 egg, lightly beaten
- 1 deep-dish 9-inch frozen pie shell, thawed

1. Heat oven to 375°.
2. Melt 2 tablespoons butter in large heavy saucepan. Stir in apples. Stir in $1/2$ cup granulated sugar; cook, stirring frequently, 12 to 15 minutes or until barely tender. Stir in $1/2$ teaspoon vanilla. Remove from heat.
3. Streusel topping: Combine walnuts, brown sugar, $1/2$ cup flour, cinnamon and half the salt in a small bowl. With fingertips, rub 6 tablespoons butter into flour mixture until crumbly.
4. Mix sour cream, remaining granulated sugar, salt, flour and vanilla in a medium bowl. Mix in nutmeg and egg.
5. Drain apples in colander; fold into sour cream mixture. Spoon into pie shell; tilt slightly so liquid flows evenly to all parts of pie shell. Sprinkle streusel topping on apple filling. Place on baking sheet.
6. Bake in 375° oven for 50 to 60 minutes or until apples are fork-tender. If the streusel topping starts to brown too quickly, loosely tent the pie with aluminum foil for the last 20 minutes of baking. Let pie cool for at least 4 hours before serving.
Yield: 10 servings.
Make-Ahead Tip: Can be made a day ahead. Cover pie and refrigerate.

PUMPKIN CARAMEL FLAN

- $3/4$ cup granulated sugar
- $1/2$ cup firmly packed light-brown sugar
- $1/2$ cup canned solid-pack pumpkin purée (not pie filling)
- 6 eggs
- 2 cups milk
- 1 teaspoon vanilla
- $3/4$ teaspoon ground allspice OR ground cinnamon
  Mint leaves or grapes, for garnish (optional)

1. Heat oven to 325°. Set eight 6-ounce custard cups nearby.
2. Heat granulated sugar in heavy skillet or saucepan over medium heat until sugar melts and caramelizes to a golden amber color.
3. Spoon caramel into custard cups, tilting to coat bottoms and 1 inch up sides. Place in large roasting pan.
4. Whisk together brown sugar, pumpkin, eggs, milk, vanilla and allspice in large bowl. Divide equally among custard cups. Pour enough simmering water into roasting pan to come halfway up sides of cups.
5. Bake in 325° oven for 50 minutes or until knife inserted in centers comes out clean. Remove cups from water to wire rack. Cool slightly. Refrigerate overnight.
6. To serve, run a small spatula around edge of each cup. Invert onto serving dishes, shaking to release. Scrape any remaining caramel from cups onto flan. Garnish with mint leaves or grapes, if you wish.
Yield: 8 servings.

MAPLE-PEAR TART TATIN

- 1/4 cup plus 2 tablespoons firmly packed dark-brown sugar
- 2 cans (15 1/4 ounces each) pear halves, in syrup
- 1 prepared single-crust pie pastry
- 1/4 cup pecans, finely chopped

1. Heat oven to 425°. Sprinkle 1/4 cup brown sugar over bottom of 10-inch nonstick skillet. Drain pear halves; blot dry on paper toweling.

2. Place 10 pear halves, cut side up, in circle in skillet. Fill center with remaining pears. Sprinkle remaining brown sugar over pears.

3. Roll out crust to an 11-inch circle. Spread nuts over crust. Using rolling pin, press nuts into crust; be careful not to tear crust.

4. Invert crust, nut side down, onto pears in skillet. Tuck crust overlap between pears and edge of pan, forming lip.

5. Bake in 425° oven 25 minutes or until crust is golden. Transfer skillet to wire rack; let stand 15 minutes or until pan is cool enough to handle. Invert serving platter on top of skillet; flip tart onto platter.

Yield: 8 servings.

Make-Ahead Tip: Tart can be made a few hours before serving. Let stand, loosely covered, at room temperature.

H alf-moon-shaped Mini Calzones hide a pleasing three-cheese filling, while Bruschetta, the toasted Italian bread starter, takes well to any of three tempting toppings: White Bean with Olive, Onion-Rosemary or Tomato-Basil.

tasty tidbits

Stave off the hungries and kick-start a **party**
mood with simply scrumptious appetizers that hint at
good things yet to come. Best of all — you won't be
stuck in the kitchen with loads of prep work!

MINI CALZONES

- 1/4 cup shredded reduced-fat mozzarella cheese
- 1/4 cup ricotta cheese
- 2 tablespoons grated Parmesan cheese
- 1/2 teaspoon bottled pesto
- 2 slices smoked turkey (1 ounce total), diced
- 2 teaspoons chopped fresh basil OR 1/8 teaspoon dried basil
- 1/8 teaspoon ground black pepper
- 2 packages (about 10 ounces each) refrigerated pizza dough
- 1 egg, lightly beaten

1. Heat oven to 425°. Mix cheeses, pesto, turkey, basil and pepper in bowl.
2. Press both packages of dough flat; cut 20 rounds, using 2³/₄-inch cookie cutter. Brush edges with beaten egg. Place 1 level teaspoon cheese filling in center of each round. Fold in half; seal edges; crimp with fingers. Brush egg over sealed calzones. Place on greased baking sheet.
3. Bake in 425° oven 10 to 12 minutes or until golden and glazed. Cool slightly before serving.
Yield: 20 calzones.

3-WAY BRUSCHETTA

- 2 loaves Italian bread Onion-Rosemary, Tomato-Basil and White Bean with Olive Toppings (recipes follow)

Heat broiler. Slice each loaf on diagonal into 18 slices. Toast 2 to 3 minutes per side, turning once. Spoon on toppings. Serve immediately.

ONION-ROSEMARY TOPPING

- 2 small yellow onions, sliced in thin rings
- 2 tablespoons butter
- 3 tablespoons water (optional)
- 1/4 teaspoon salt
- 1/8 teaspoon ground black pepper
- 2 teaspoons red-wine vinegar
- 1 teaspoon chopped fresh rosemary OR 1/4 teaspoon dried rosemary
- 1/3 cup ricotta cheese
- 12 slices Bruschetta toast

Sauté onions in butter in skillet until softened, 10 minutes; add water, if needed. Add salt, pepper, vinegar and rosemary; cook 2 minutes. Spread ricotta on toast. Top with onions.
Yield: 12 slices.

TOMATO-BASIL TOPPING

- 3 large plum tomatoes, diced
- 2 cloves garlic, chopped
- 2 tablespoons chopped fresh basil
- 1 tablespoon balsamic vinegar
- 1 tablespoon olive oil
- 1/8 teaspoon salt
- 1/8 teaspoon ground black pepper
- 12 slices Bruschetta toast

Mix all ingredients, except toast, in bowl. Spoon on toast.
Yield: 12 slices.

WHITE BEAN-OLIVE TOPPING

- 1 can (10.5 ounces) white cannellini beans, drained and rinsed
- 10 Kalamata olives, pitted and chopped
- 1 tablespoon chopped fresh parsley
- 1 tablespoon olive oil
- 1 tablespoon lemon juice
- 1/4 teaspoon salt
- 1/8 teaspoon ground black pepper
- 12 slices Bruschetta toast

Mash beans. Add remaining ingredients, except toast, in bowl; mix. Spread on toast.
Yield: 12 slices.

SAVORY CREAM PUFFS

1 cup milk
1/2 cup (1 stick) butter or margarine
1/4 teaspoon salt
1 cup all-purpose flour
2 eggs
3 egg whites
   Savory Prosciutto OR Tomato-
   Olive Flavoring (recipes follow)

1. Heat oven to 450°.
2. Heat milk, butter and salt in medium-size saucepan. As soon as mixture comes to boiling, remove from heat. Immediately stir in flour with wooden spoon; beat until dough pulls away from sides of pan.
3. Beat in eggs and egg whites, one at a time, beating after each addition, until mixture is smooth and glossy. Stir in Savory Prosciutto Flavoring or Tomato-Olive Flavoring.

4. Place mounds of dough (about the size of a large walnut) on prepared baking sheets, 1 1/2 inches apart. Or pipe from pastry bag, fitted with desired tip, onto greased baking sheets.
5. Place in upper third of 450° oven. Reduce oven temperature to 400°. Bake 25 minutes or until puffed, golden and lightly crusty. Remove to wire racks.
Yield: 3 1/2 dozen puffs.
Savory Prosciutto Flavoring: Combine 1/2 cup grated Parmesan cheese, 1/4 cup finely chopped prosciutto and 1/4 teaspoon ground nutmeg in a small bowl.
Tomato-Olive Flavoring: Plump 1 ounce dry-pack sun-dried tomatoes in hot water for 20 minutes; finely chop. Combine tomatoes with 2 tablespoons finely chopped canned black olives in a small bowl.
Make-Ahead Tip: The baked puffs can be frozen. To reheat, place on baking sheet. Cover lightly with aluminum foil. Bake in preheated 375° oven for 10 minutes.

WARM CLAM DIP

8 ounces reduced-fat cream cheese
8 ounces nonfat cream cheese
2 tablespoons nonfat milk
3 cans (6.5 ounces each) minced clams, 1 can undrained and 2 cans drained
1/2 cup chopped green onions
1 tablespoon fresh lemon juice
1/4 teaspoon hot-pepper sauce
1 cup finely crushed reduced-fat buttery crackers (about 24 crackers)
   Reduced-fat buttery crackers for serving

1. Heat oven to 350°.
2. Beat cream cheeses and milk in large bowl on medium speed until fluffy. Add 1 undrained can and 2 drained cans of clams, green onions, lemon juice and hot sauce; beat on low until combined. Stir in crackers. Scrape clam mixture into 4-cup ovenproof serving dish.
3. Bake in 350° oven 30 minutes or until center is set. Serve warm.
Yield: 16 servings.

FLAVORED CHEESES

2 packages (7 ounces each) farmer
    cheese
    Assorted bread party rounds and
    crackers for serving

Lemon Cheese:

2 tablespoons cream cheese
1 tablespoon grated lemon zest
1 tablespoon fresh lemon juice
1 teaspoon sugar
$^1/_2$ teaspoon salt
$^1/_8$ teaspoon ground black pepper
    Strips of lemon zest
    Chopped fresh parsley

Great Garlic Cheese:

2 tablespoons cream cheese
2 tablespoons dried rubbed sage
1 to 2 cloves garlic, finely chopped
1 teaspoon red-wine vinegar
$^1/_2$ teaspoon salt
$^1/_8$ teaspoon ground black pepper
    Fresh sage leaves

1. Prepare Lemon Cheese: Place
1 package of farmer cheese, cream
cheese, lemon zest, lemon juice, sugar,
salt and pepper in food processor. Pulse
until smooth. Scoop cheese into a small
serving bowl. Garnish with lemon zest
and chopped fresh parsley.

2. Prepare Great Garlic Cheese: Place
second package of farmer cheese, cream
cheese, sage, garlic, red-wine vinegar,
salt and pepper in food processor. Pulse
at high speed until smooth. Scoop
cheese into a small serving bowl.
Garnish with sage leaves.

3. Serve the cheeses at room
temperature with bread rounds
and crackers.

Yield: 12 servings.

*Savory Cream Puffs (opposite, top) are a lifesaver — just make them in
advance, freeze, then reheat before serving. Canned clams turn Warm Clam Dip
(left) into a skinny, simple-to-do specialty. Serve our Flavored Cheeses (above)
with an array of crackers and breads or as dips with crunchy crudités.*

resh lime juice lends *Caramelized Onion Quesadillas a real kick. Though leftovers are unlikely, they can be microwaved for snacks. With a tempting three-cheese combination, Warm Cheddar-Thyme Vidalia dip (opposite, top) is extra-pleasing. Our irresistible Barbecue Wings (opposite, bottom) are a sweet-and-sour classic: honey for the sweet and red-wine vinegar for the sour. Hot-pepper sauce delivers a touch of pizzazz.*

CARAMELIZED ONION QUESADILLAS

- 1 tablespoon olive oil
- 1 red onion, halved and thinly sliced crosswise
- 4 scallions, sliced
- 3 cloves garlic, chopped
- 3/4 teaspoon ground cumin
- 1/4 teaspoon dried oregano, crumbled
- 1 tablespoon fresh lime juice
- 4 large (10-inch) flour tortillas
- 1 cup shredded jalapeño-Jack cheese (4 ounces)
- 1 cup shredded sharp Cheddar cheese (4 ounces)
  Bottled salsa (optional)
  Sour cream (optional)

1. Heat oil in skillet over medium-low heat. Add red onion, scallions and garlic; cook, covered, stirring occasionally, until softened, about 15 minutes.
2. Add cumin and oregano; cook, uncovered, 1 minute. Remove from heat. Stir in lime juice.
3. Heat oven to 400°.
4. Place 2 tortillas side-by-side on baking sheet. Divide onion mixture between each tortilla. Sprinkle each with cheeses. Top each with remaining tortillas.
5. Bake in 400° oven 8 minutes or until heated through and tortillas are golden around edges. Let stand 5 minutes. Cut each into sixths. Serve with salsa and sour cream, if you wish.
Yield: 4 servings.

WARM CHEDDAR-THYME VIDALIA DIP

- 1 large Vidalia onion or other sweet onion (about 1 pound), finely chopped (3 cups)
- 6 ounces pepper-Jack cheese, shredded
- 6 ounces reduced-fat Cheddar cheese, shredded
- 4 ounces reduced-fat cream cheese
- 1/2 cup reduced-fat mayonnaise
- 1 teaspoon fresh thyme leaves, chopped OR 1/4 teaspoon dried thyme

Crackers or toast for serving

1. Heat oven to 375°.
2. Place 2 cups onion in a bowl.
3. Combine shredded cheeses, cream cheese, mayonnaise, thyme and remaining 1 cup onion in food processor. Process until fairly smooth. Mix with finely chopped onion in bowl. Spoon into shallow 6-cup baking dish.
4. Bake in 375° oven 20 minutes. Stir. Bake 10 minutes. Cool slightly. Serve with crackers or toast.
Yield: 16 servings.

BARBECUE WINGS

- 2 1/2 pounds chicken wings
- 3/4 cup chili sauce
- 2 tablespoons honey
- 2 tablespoons soy sauce
- 2 teaspoons dry mustard
- 1 teaspoon red-wine vinegar
- 5 drops hot-pepper sauce
- 2 scallions, sliced
- 1 teaspoon salt

1. Heat oven to 375°. Grease large baking pan.
2. Cut off wing tips; save for soup or stock. Cut wings in half at joint.
3. Combine chili sauce, honey, soy sauce, mustard, vinegar, pepper sauce, scallions and salt in large bowl. Add wings; toss to coat. Place wings in baking pan.
4. Bake in 375° oven for 45 minutes, turning every 15 minutes.
5. Set oven to broil. Broil wings until crisp, 2 to 3 minutes per side.
Yield: 6 servings.

CRISPY CROQUETTES

    2   teaspoons vegetable oil
    1   medium-size onion, finely chopped
    1   medium-size carrot, peeled and
        finely chopped
    1   small white potato, peeled and cut
        into 1/4-inch cubes
    1/2 cup chicken broth
    1/2 cup all-purpose flour
    2/3 cup milk
    1   tablespoon chopped fresh parsley
    1/8 teaspoon salt
    1 1/4 cups dry bread crumbs
    6   ounces diced Spanish Serrano
        ham OR prosciutto
    2/3 cup grated manchego cheese OR
        grated Parmesan cheese
    2   eggs
    3/4 cup vegetable oil, for frying

1. Heat 2 teaspoons oil in small saucepan. Add onion, carrot and potato; sauté for 5 minutes or until slightly softened. Add broth; cover and cook 5 minutes.

2. Meanwhile, whisk together flour, milk, parsley and salt in small bowl. Whisk flour mixture and 1/4 cup bread crumbs into vegetable mixture in saucepan. Cook for 2 minutes, whisking occasionally; mixture will be thick. Remove from heat. Stir in ham and cheese. Refrigerate until cool to touch and scoopable in texture, about 30 minutes.

3. Whisk eggs in small bowl. Spread remaining 1 cup bread crumbs in shallow dish. Using measuring tablespoon, scoop filling into 1-inch balls, rolling between

hands coated with nonstick vegetable-oil cooking spray. Dip croquettes into egg, then in bread crumbs to coat.

4. Heat frying oil in 8-inch skillet over medium-high heat. Working in batches, fry about 3 minutes per batch or until golden all around outside. Serve hot.
Yield: 8 servings.

Each Crispy Croquette (above) offers an appealing burst of aged cheese and Serrano ham. Accent these delicious Ham Skewers (right) with garlic-and-lemon-laced aioli.

HAM SKEWERS WITH PINK AIOLI

- $^3/_4$ pound red or white new potatoes, quartered
- 3 cloves garlic, pressed or mashed
- $^3/_4$ cup mayonnaise
- 1 teaspoon olive oil
- 1 tablespoon lemon juice
- $^1/_8$ teaspoon salt
- $^1/_8$ teaspoon ground black pepper
- 1 jar (7 ounces) roasted red peppers, drained
- $^1/_2$ pound ham (whole piece), cut into 1-inch cubes

1. Prepare outdoor grill with hot coals, heat gas grill to hot, or heat broiler. Soak eighteen 8-inch wooden skewers in warm water, while preparing food, to prevent scorching during cooking.

2. Place potatoes in medium-size saucepan with enough water to cover. Bring to boiling; cook 7 minutes or until barely tender. Drain; rinse. Let cool so pieces do not split while threading skewers.

3. Prepare aioli: Combine garlic, mayonnaise, olive oil, lemon juice, salt and pepper in food processor or blender.

Chop about 3 tablespoons of roasted peppers and add to blender. Pureé until smooth and blended.

4. Once potatoes have cooled, remove soaked skewers from water. Thread each skewer with 1 ham cube. Slice remaining peppers into 1-inch pieces. Thread onto skewers, followed by potato. (Skewers may be prepared up to this point and refrigerated.)

5. Grill or broil for 3 minutes, turning once. Serve skewers with pink aioli sauce.
Yield: 6 servings.

Santa's little helpers

Candies, lollipops and fudge … oh my! Even wee ones can create these **yummy** goodies (with a little help from you). Make enough of each to allow for frequent taste tests!

CHOCO-BERRY ROUNDS

Experiment with other jellies such as strawberry, currant and blackberry.

- $\frac{1}{2}$ cup (1 stick) butter, at room temperature
- $2\frac{1}{2}$ cups sifted confectioners' sugar
- $\frac{2}{3}$ cup sifted unsweetened cocoa powder
- 2 tablespoons raspberry jelly, melted
- 1 tablespoon heavy cream
  Nonpareils, sugars, jimmies or other decorations

1. Beat butter in large bowl until light and fluffy, about 3 minutes. Add confectioners' sugar, cocoa powder, jelly and cream; beat until well blended and dough forms.
2. Cover dough and refrigerate about 2 hours or until firm enough to roll into balls.
3. Using tablespoonfuls of dough, shape mixture into 1-inch balls. Place on waxed-paper-lined 15 x 10 x 1-inch baking pan. Refrigerate 30 minutes.
4. Roll balls in decorations, as desired. Return to refrigerator to chill until ready to serve. Store in refrigerator for up to 1 week.
Yield: About $2\frac{1}{2}$ dozen candies.

ROCKY ROAD CLUSTERS

Leave a couple of these out for Santa, and you're bound to get some extra gifts!

- 1 can (14 ounces) sweetened condensed milk
- 1 package (12 ounces) semisweet chocolate chips
- 1 cup dry-roasted peanuts
- 1 cup butterscotch-brickle bits OR 3 packages (2.5 ounces each) chocolate-covered butterscotch bits
- $1\frac{1}{2}$ teaspoons vanilla
- 2 cups mini marshmallows

1. Line 3 large baking sheets with waxed paper.
2. Mix condensed milk and chocolate chips in 2-quart microwave-safe bowl. Microwave at full power (100%) for $2\frac{1}{2}$ to 3 minutes or until chocolate melts, stirring twice. Stir in peanuts, butterscotch bits and vanilla. Cool slightly. Fold in the marshmallows.
3. Drop batter by rounded measuring tablespoons onto prepared baking sheets. Refrigerate until firm, about 15 to 20 minutes.
4. Store clusters in airtight container at room temperature for up to 1 week.
Yield: $2\frac{1}{2}$ to 3 dozen candies.

Rocky Road Clusters *(left) burst with kids' favorites: butterscotch, chocolate chips, marshmallows and peanuts. After you've finished mixing, little ones can drop the batter onto baking pans by the spoonful — the chunkier, the better!* Choco-Berry Rounds *(above) really get small fry rockin'! First, they roll the jelly-and-cocoa mixture into balls, then roll 'em in holiday sugars, jimmies or nonpareils.*

Squiggle melted white chocolate onto each Festive Fudge square (below), *using a plastic bag with a corner snipped off. For our Coconut Trees (opposite), youngsters mold a green-tinted confection into cones, then trim with tiny candies. To make them portable, poke a lollipop stick in each. Even preschoolers can help shape ooey-gooey Popcorn Balls (not pictured).*

FESTIVE FUDGE

Almonds or macadamias are delicious alternatives to pecans.

1 package (11.5 ounces) milk-chocolate chips
1 can (14 ounces) sweetened condensed milk
1 cup chopped toasted pecans
1 teaspoon vanilla
1/2 cup white-chocolate baking chips, melted (optional)

1. Line an 8-inch square pan with aluminum foil. Mix chocolate chips and milk in bowl. Microwave at full power (100%) for 3 minutes, stirring every minute. Add nuts and vanilla. Pour into pan. Cool slightly. Refrigerate 2 hours, until firm.
2. Drizzle with white chocolate, if desired. Chill until firm.
3. Remove fudge from the foil. Cut into 1-inch squares.
4. Store in airtight container for up to 2 weeks.
Yield: About 64 pieces.

COCONUT TREES

You can never have too many little hands helping to decorate these tasty mini trees.

- 8 ounces (1⅓ cups) green candy coating disks
- 2 tablespoons water
- 1 tablespoon light corn syrup
- 2 cups sweetened flake coconut
  Nonpareils, sugars, jimmies or other decorations (optional)
  Lollipop sticks (optional)

1. Heat disks, water and corn syrup in heavy medium-size saucepan over low heat until mixture is smooth, about 10 minutes. Stir in coconut.
2. When mixture is cool enough to handle, shape level measuring tablespoonfuls into cones about 1½ inches high. Place on waxed paper. Decorate as desired. Insert sticks in bottom, if using. Set aside until firm.
3. Store in airtight container for up to 1 week.
Yield: 20 trees.

POPCORN BALLS

They make great stocking stuffers!

- 3 quarts (12 cups) freshly popped popcorn
- 2 cups salted dry-roasted peanuts
- 1 cup firmly packed dark-brown sugar
- ½ cup light molasses
- ½ teaspoon white vinegar

1. Combine popped popcorn and peanuts in large bowl.
2. Heat brown sugar, molasses and vinegar in heavy saucepan over low heat, stirring often, until candy thermometer registers 250° (hard-ball stage), about 30 minutes. Pour over popcorn; toss with large spoons to coat.
3. Butter hands and 1-cup dry measuring cup. While mixture is still warm, scoop rounded cupfuls onto waxed paper. Press into balls. Wrap each in plastic wrap.
4. Store in airtight container at room temperature for up to 2 weeks.
Yield: About 12 balls.

ALMOND BUTTER CRUNCH

Steady hands are needed to spread chocolate over the candy.

- 1 cup (2 sticks) butter
- 1¹/₂ cups firmly packed light-brown sugar
- 3 tablespoons water
- 1 tablespoon light corn syrup
- 1 package (11.5 ounces) milk-chocolate chips
- 8 ounces (1¹/₂ cups) whole blanched almonds, toasted and finely ground

1. Butter large baking sheet. Bring butter, brown sugar, water and corn syrup to boiling in heavy medium-size saucepan over medium-high heat, about 10 minutes. Cook until candy thermometer registers 300° (hard-crack stage), about 15 minutes. Remove from heat; stir for 1 minute. Immediately pour mixture onto prepared baking sheet. As it cools, use thin metal spatula to push into 13 x 9-inch rectangle. Cool.
2. Melt 1 cup chocolate chips in double boiler over hot water. Spread over candy on baking sheet. Sprinkle with half the nuts, pressing into chocolate.
3. After chocolate sets, cover with waxed paper and a second baking sheet. Invert candy onto waxed paper. Repeat Step 2. Let stand until chocolate is firm. Break into pieces.
4. Store in refrigerator for up to 2 weeks.
Yield: 2 pounds.

NOUGAT BARS

The edible rice paper used in this recipe is available in stores specializing in candy-making supplies.

- 3 egg whites
- 2 sheets edible rice paper Confectioners' sugar
- 2¹/₄ cups sugar
- 1 cup light corn syrup
- ¹/₂ cup water
- ¹/₄ cup honey
- 3 tablespoons butter, melted
- 1 teaspoon almond extract
- 1 pound (3 cups) whole unblanched almonds

1. Let egg whites come to room temperature in large bowl, about 1 hour.
2. Cut rice paper to fit bottom of 11 x 7 x 2-inch (2-quart) baking dish. Line bottom of dish with heavy-duty aluminum foil. Coat dish sides with nonstick vegetable-oil cooking spray. Dust with confectioners' sugar. Place 1 sheet of cut rice paper on foil.
3. Bring sugar, corn syrup and water to boiling in saucepan over medium-high heat, stirring occasionally, about 8 minutes. Cook, without stirring, until a candy thermometer registers 275° (soft-crack stage), about 25 minutes.
4. On high speed of an electric mixer, beat egg whites until stiff peaks form.
5. Microwave honey in glass measuring cup at full power (100%) until boiling, about 30 seconds. With mixer running, slowly add the honey to whites and continue beating for 1 to 2 minutes, until doubled in volume. With mixer running, slowly add sugar syrup and beat until light and airy, about 7 to 8 minutes. Beat in butter and almond extract. Fold in nuts.
6. Immediately spread the mixture in prepared pan. Top with second sheet rice paper. Chill several hours to firm.
7. Remove candy from pan. Peel off foil and paper. Cut into 2 x 1-inch bars. Wrap each piece in plastic wrap.
8. Store in refrigerator for up to 1 week.
Yield: 35 bars.

CHOCOLATE-PEANUT BUTTER BARS

Chocolate and peanut butter — who could resist?

- 2¹/₂ cups chocolate graham-cracker crumbs (17 whole crackers)
- 2¹/₂ cups confectioners' sugar
- 1 cup creamy peanut butter
- 1 cup (2 sticks) butter, melted
- 1 bag (12 ounces) semisweet chocolate chips
- 75 red and green candy-coated chocolate-covered-peanut candies

1. Line 15 x 10 x 1-inch baking pan with aluminum foil.
2. Stir together graham-cracker crumbs, sugar, peanut butter and butter in large bowl. Press evenly in prepared pan.
3. Melt chocolate in saucepan over low heat. Pour over mixture in pan; spread evenly. Chill 20 minutes, until slightly firm. Score in pan into 2 x 1-inch bars. Press 1 candy into top of each. Cut through bars along lines. Chill to firm. Remove from pan.
4. Store in refrigerator for up to 2 weeks.
Yield: 75 bars.

These dreamy concoctions are almost too good to be true. (Opposite, clockwise from top:) No-bake Chocolate-Peanut Butter Bars are oh-so-simple to make — kids can do most of the prep work and top each with a candy-coated peanut. Chewy Nougat Bars are chock-full of toasty almonds. Let children fold in the nuts and spread the mixture in a baking dish. Almond Butter Crunch lives up to its name in each rich, nutty bite. A bonus: the milk-chocolate topping. Because our butter-crunch recipe requires careful cooking, it's best if Mom handles that task. But almost anyone can slather the melted chocolate around.

Classic Christmas Desserts

a sugary **indulgence**, presented on your best server, elevates
even the most casual celebration into an affair to remember.
Try any one of our **luscious** desserts for a glorious grand-finale.

BÛCHE DE NOËL

- 1 cup unsifted cake flour
- 1/4 cup unsweetened cocoa powder
- 1 teaspoon baking powder
- 1/4 teaspoon salt
- 3 eggs
- 1 cup granulated sugar
- 1/3 cup water
- 1 teaspoon vanilla
  Confectioners' sugar
  Coffee-Cream Filling (recipe follows)
  Chocolate Butter Frosting (recipe follows)
- 1/4 cup chopped pistachio nuts
  Chocolate Curls and Meringue Mushrooms (recipes, this page)

1. Heat oven to 375°. Line a greased 15 x 10 x 1-inch jelly-roll pan with waxed paper; grease again.
2. Sift together flour, cocoa, baking powder and salt. In small bowl with mixer at high speed, beat eggs until thick and creamy.
3. Beat in granulated sugar, 1 tablespoon at a time, until mixture is very thick. Stir in water and vanilla; fold in flour mixture. Spread batter evenly in prepared pan.
4. Bake in preheated 375° oven 12 minutes, until center springs back when lightly pressed with fingertip.
5. Loosen cake around edges of pan with sharp knife; invert pan onto clean towel dusted with confectioners' sugar; peel off waxed paper. Starting at long side, roll up cake, jelly-roll fashion; wrap in towel, Cool completely.
6. Unroll cake carefully. Spread with the Coffee-Cream Filling; reroll.
7. For each knot, cut 1/2-inch-thick slice from 1 end of cake. Cut out inner coil and reroll remainder of slice tightly to form "knot" for log; frost with Chocolate Butter Frosting.
8. Cover log with remaining frosting;

draw tines of fork lengthwise through frosting to create "bark." Press frosted "knots" onto log. Sprinkle ends of log with chopped pistachio nuts. Chill until serving time. Decorate with Chocolate Curls and Meringue Mushrooms.
Coffee-Cream Filling: In medium-size bowl, combine 1 cup heavy cream, 1 tablespoon instant-coffee powder and 1/2 cup confectioners' sugar. With electric mixer at medium speed, beat mixture until stiff. Makes 2 cups.
Chocolate Butter Frosting: In small saucepan, melt 1/4 cup (1/2 stick) butter or margarine and 2 squares unsweetened chocolate; cool slightly. Add 2 cups confectioners' sugar, 1/4 cup milk and 1/2 teaspoon vanilla. Beat until smooth.
Yield: 12 servings.

CHOCOLATE CURLS

- 1 package (12 ounces) semisweet chocolate chips
- 1 tablespoon solid vegetable shortening

1. Line 2 large baking sheets with waxed paper. Then line 8 1/2 x 4 1/2 x 2-inch loaf pan with sheet of aluminum foil.
2. In a small heavy-bottomed saucepan, melt chocolate chips and vegetable shortening over medium heat, stirring until smooth. Pour into prepared loaf pan. Refrigerate 1 hour or just until firm in center. (If too firm, chocolate will not curl.)
3. Turn out chocolate onto pastry board, and cut in half lengthwise, then crosswise, making 4 "bars." Scrape a swivel-bladed vegetable peeler lengthwise across bars for curls.
4. Lift curls off peeler blade with wooden pick; set on prepared baking sheets. Refrigerate for at least 30 minutes before using. If bars soften, chill until firm enough to handle. Wipe peeler blade frequently to prevent chocolate from sticking.

MERINGUE MUSHROOMS

- 2 egg whites
- 1/8 teaspoon cream of tartar
- 1/2 teaspoon almond extract
- 2/3 cup sugar
- 1/4 cup semisweet chocolate chips
  Cocoa powder, for garnish (optional)

1. Heat oven to 250°. Grease 2 large baking sheets; flour lightly, tapping out excess flour.
2. Beat egg whites, cream of tartar, and almond extract in a small bowl at high speed of an electric mixer until soft peaks form.
3. Sprinkle in sugar, 1 tablespoon at a time, beating until sugar dissolves and stiff peaks form.
4. Spoon meringue into pastry bag fitted with large round tip.
5. For mushroom caps, press out meringue onto 1 baking sheet to make twenty-four 1 1/2-inch rounds. Smooth top of each cap, if needed, with a knife, but do not flatten.
6. Hold pastry bag upright and press out meringue onto other baking sheet, pulling straight up on the bag, to make twenty-four 1 1/2-inch mushroom stems.
7. Bake in preheated 250° oven 30 minutes or until firm but not brown. Let stand for several minutes on baking sheets. Loosen caps and stems carefully with small knife; transfer to wire racks with spatula. Cool completely.
8. Melt chocolate in a small heavy-bottomed saucepan over low heat.
9. Working carefully, make a small hollow in the underside of each cap. Add dab of melted chocolate to hollow; press 1 stem into hollow. Repeat with remaining caps and stems. Let stand until chocolate is firm.
10. Sprinkle tops of mushrooms with cocoa powder, if desired. Store in a tightly covered container in a cool, dry place.

Bûche de Noël filled with coffee cream is always a crowd-pleaser. Be sure to serve each slice with a cocoa-dusted Meringue Mushroom.

Satisfy a sweet tooth with ice-cream-filled Peppermint Profiteroles (right, from top) or Bittersweet Chocolate Cakes — dark chocolate is at its ultrarichest in these tiny treats, while our pint-sized puffs offer a frosty burst of mint. Glacéed cherries and red food coloring make Cherry Stacks (opposite) a cheery snack.

BITTERSWEET CHOCOLATE CAKES

Cakes:

2	cups all-purpose flour
$2/3$	cup unsweetened cocoa powder
$1^1/2$	teaspoons ground cinnamon
1	teaspoon baking powder
1	teaspoon baking soda
$1/2$	teaspoon salt
$1/4$	teaspoon ground nutmeg
1	cup (2 sticks) butter, at room temperature
$1^1/2$	cups firmly packed light-brown sugar
3	eggs
2	teaspoons vanilla
$1^1/2$	cups sour cream
5	ounces bittersweet chocolate, chopped
1	cup almonds, chopped

Ganache Frosting:

$2^1/4$	cups heavy cream
1	pound 2 ounces bittersweet chocolate, chopped
	Sliced almonds, for garnish (optional)

1. Prepare Cakes: Heat oven to 350°. With nonstick vegetable-oil cooking spray, coat standard-size muffin pan with $2^1/2$ x 1-inch cups (see Note).
2. Combine flour, cocoa powder, cinnamon, baking powder, baking soda, salt and nutmeg in large bowl.
3. In another large bowl, beat butter on medium speed of an electric mixer until smooth, about 1 minute. Gradually beat in sugar; then beat on medium-high 3 minutes or until fluffy. Add eggs, 1 at a time, beating well after each addition. Beat in vanilla. On low speed, beat in flour mixture alternately with sour cream in 3 additions, beginning and ending with flour; beat 2 minutes. Fold in chocolate and nuts. Fill muffin cups half-full.
4. Bake in 350° oven 15 minutes or until tops spring back when touched. Cool cakes in pan on wire rack 10 minutes. Turn cakes out onto rack; cool. Repeat with rest of batter.
5. Prepare Ganache: Bring cream to boiling in small saucepan. Place chocolate in small bowl. Pour hot cream over chocolate; stir until smooth.

6. Place wire racks over jelly-roll pan. Place cakes with large, flat-side down, on racks. Pour about 2 tablespoons ganache evenly over each cake to cover completely; smooth ganache with small spatula.
7. Garnish each cake with 2 or 3 almonds, if desired. Refrigerate for 1 hour or until ganache is firm.
Yield: 36 cakes.
Note: For larger cakes, use oversize muffin cups, $3^1/2$ x $1^3/4$ inch. Bake 25 minutes. For ganache, use 12 ounces bittersweet chocolate and $1^1/2$ cups heavy cream. Makes 12 cakes.

PEPPERMINT PROFITEROLES

- 1 cup water
- ½ cup (1 stick) butter
- 1 teaspoon sugar
- ¼ teaspoon salt
- 1 cup all-purpose flour
- 4 eggs
- 2 pints vanilla ice cream
- ½ teaspoon peppermint extract
- 4 tablespoons crushed candy canes (about three 5½-inch candy canes)
  Red and green chocolate disks for drizzle

1. Heat oven to 400°.
2. Bring water, butter, sugar and salt in saucepan to boiling over high heat. Add flour all at once; stir with wooden spoon until mixture forms a ball that pulls away from side of pan. Cook another 2 minutes, stirring continuously.
3. Remove from heat. Add eggs, one at a time, beating well with a wooden spoon after each addition. When all eggs have been added, continue to beat until shiny.

4. Scrape flour mixture into large pastry bag without tip. Pipe 12 equal puffs, about 2 inches in diameter, onto ungreased baking sheet, spacing about 2 inches apart.
5. Bake in 400° oven for 35 minutes or until puffed and golden. Turn oven off. Let puffs stand in oven 10 minutes with the door slightly ajar. Transfer to wire rack to cool completely.
6. Transfer ice cream to bowl; let soften. Stir in peppermint extract and crushed candy canes. Cover; return to freezer.
7. Cut cooled puffs in half horizontally; remove any wet dough from centers. Using 2½-inch ice-cream scoop, place scoop of peppermint ice cream on each puff bottom. Place puff top on each ice-cream ball. Place in freezer.
8. Melt red and green chocolate disks separately in small saucepans over low heat. Drizzle over each profiterole. Return to freezer to harden before serving.
Yield: 12 profiteroles.

CHERRY STACKS
Cake:
- 1¼ cups all-purpose flour
- ½ teaspoon baking powder
- ¼ teaspoon salt
- 3 tablespoons unsalted butter
- 3 tablespoons margarine
- ½ cup sugar
- ¼ cup almond paste
- 1 egg
- 2 tablespoons milk
- ½ teaspoon almond extract

Cherry Layers:
  Red food coloring
- ½ cup finely chopped glacé cherries

Assembly:
- ½ cup strained apricot preserves
- 3 ounces semisweet chocolate

1. Heat oven to 350°.
2. Grease three 13 x 9 x 2-inch pans; line with waxed paper; grease paper.
3. Prepare White Cake Layer: Stir together flour, baking powder and salt.
4. Beat together butter, margarine, sugar, and almond paste in bowl until creamy. Beat in egg, milk, and almond extract until well blended. Stir in flour mixture.
5. Spread batter in 1 prepared pan. Bake in 350° oven 15 minutes. Let cool in pan on rack 10 minutes. Carefully remove from pan; peel off paper. Cool.
6. Prepare Cherry Layers: Prepare double Cake recipe. Mix in red food coloring, and ½ cup finely chopped glacé cherries. Spread half the batter in each remaining pan. Bake in 350° oven 15 minutes. Let cool in pans on rack 10 minutes. Carefully remove from pans; peel off paper. Cool.
7. Assembly: Place 1 pink cake on baking sheet. Spread top with ¼ cup strained apricot preserves. Top with white cake. Spread with ¼ cup strained apricot preserves. Top with remaining pink layer. Cover cake and weight down with a heavy cutting board overnight. Melt 3 ounces semisweet chocolate. Spread over top. Let stand to harden. Cut into 1-inch squares.
Yield: About 9 dozen.

FOUR-LAYER SPICE CAKE

Cake:

2½ cups all-purpose flour
1 tablespoon baking powder
2 teaspoons ground cinnamon
1 teaspoon ground nutmeg
1 teaspoon ground ginger
½ teaspoon ground cloves
½ teaspoon salt
1 cup (2 sticks) butter, at room temperature
1¼ cups firmly packed dark-brown sugar
4 eggs
1 teaspoon vanilla
1 teaspoon walnut extract
¾ cup milk
¾ cup shelled walnuts, finely chopped

Simple Syrup:

6 tablespoons dark-brown sugar
6 tablespoons water
3 tablespoons dark rum

Whipped Cream:

2 tablespoons Simple Syrup (recipe above)
1 teaspoon unflavored gelatin
2 cups heavy cream
1 teaspoon vanilla

Assembly and Garnish:

1¼ cups red glacé cherries, halved
¼ cup shelled walnut halves
Fresh mint sprigs

1. Prepare Cake: Heat oven to 350°. Coat two 8-inch round cake pans with nonstick vegetable-oil cooking spray. Line bottoms with waxed paper; coat waxed paper with cooking spray.
2. Mix flour, baking powder, cinnamon, nutmeg, ginger, cloves and salt in large bowl.

Creamy frosting and candied cherries combine for a striking stack in our Four-Layer Spice Cake (right). Now there's no need to choose between two holiday favorites — Pecan-Sweet Potato Pie (opposite) combines the best of both.

3. In another large bowl, beat together butter and sugar on medium-high speed of an electric mixer for about 3 minutes or until smooth and fluffy. Add eggs, 1 at a time, beating well after each addition. Add vanilla and walnut extracts and beat until combined. Beat in flour mixture alternately with milk in 3 additions, beginning and ending with flour, until combined; then beat for 2 minutes. Fold in nuts. Divide batter equally between prepared pans.
4. Bake in 350° oven about 30 minutes, until wooden pick inserted in centers comes out clean. Cool cakes in pans on wire rack for 10 to 15 minutes. Turn cakes out onto wire racks. Remove waxed paper from bottoms. Let cool completely on rack.
5. Prepare Simple Syrup: Stir together brown sugar and water in small heavy saucepan. Bring to boiling. Remove from heat. Stir in rum.
6. Prepare Whipped Cream: Place 2 tablespoons Simple Syrup in small dish. Sprinkle gelatin over top. Let stand until softened, about 5 minutes. Stir to dissolve gelatin, heating slightly in microwave if necessary to completely dissolve gelatin.
7. Beat cream in bowl until frothy. Add gelatin mixture and vanilla. Beat on high speed of an electric mixer until soft peaks form; use immediately.
8. Assembly and Garnish: Slice each cake layer in half horizontally to make total of four cake layers.
9. Place one layer on cake plate. Generously brush with Simple syrup. Spread 1 cup Whipped Cream over top of layer. Evenly distribute about ⅓ cup cherries over top of Whipped Cream, gently pressing cherries into cream. Repeat layering with remaining 3 cakes, syrup, Whipped Cream and cherries. Spread remaining cream over top.
10. Garnish with remaining ¼ cup cherries, walnuts and fresh mint sprigs. Refrigerate at least 1 hour before serving.
Yield: 12 servings.

PECAN-SWEET POTATO PIE

Crust:
- 1³/₄ cups all-purpose flour
- 1 teaspoon salt
- 7 tablespoons solid vegetable shortening, chilled
- ¹/₄ cup cold water

Filling:
- 1 can (15.75 ounces) cooked sweet potatoes, drained
- 4 eggs
- ¹/₃ cup firmly packed dark-brown sugar
- ¹/₂ teaspoon ground allspice
- ¹/₂ cup dark corn syrup
- ¹/₃ cup granulated sugar
- 1 teaspoon vanilla
- 1¹/₄ cups shelled pecan halves
- Whipped cream, to serve (optional)
- Vanilla ice cream, to serve (optional)

1. Prepare Crust: Mix flour and salt in large bowl. Cut in shortening with pastry blender until mixture resembles coarse cornmeal. Add water, 1 tablespoon at a time, tossing with fork, until dough comes together. Loosely shape dough into a ball. Remove one fourth of dough and shape into disk; wrap in plastic wrap. Shape remaining dough into disk; wrap. Refrigerate both disks 1 hour.
2. Roll out smaller piece of dough on waxed paper-lined baking sheet to ¹/₄-inch thickness. With 1³/₄-inch holly-leaf cookie cutter, cut out about 30 leaves. Reserve scraps. Return holly leaves to refrigerator. On lightly floured surface, roll out larger piece of dough into 12-inch round. Roll up dough on rolling pin. Unroll into 9-inch pie plate. Trim dough even with edge of rim. Refrigerate pie plate with dough.
3. Gather scraps together; roll out, ¹/₄-inch thick, on floured surface. With 1³/₄-inch maple-leaf cookie cutter, cut out about 12 maple leaves. Refrigerate.

4. Wet small area of edge of pie crust with pastry brush dipped in water. Arrange holly leaves, overlapping, along edge, moistening overlapping portions of leaves. Moisten another small section of edge of pie crust and attach leaves. Continue until edge is covered.
5. Heat oven to 350°.
6. Prepare Filling: Beat sweet potatoes, 1 egg, brown sugar and allspice in medium-size bowl 2 to 3 minutes or until smooth. Spread evenly into crust.
7. Whisk corn syrup, granulated sugar, vanilla and remaining 3 eggs in bowl until well-combined and smooth. Stir in pecans. Pour over sweet potato mixture.
8. Arrange maple leaves over top of pecan mixture.
9. Bake in 350° oven 1 hour or until filling is set and crust is light brown. Cool pie on wire rack. Serve with whipped cream or vanilla ice cream, if desired.
Yield: 10 servings.

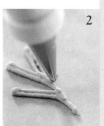

PIPING PINE NEEDLES

1. With writing tip, start needle by piping up to left, then back down with steady motion. **2.** Repeat same motion for another needle, slightly above first; then make center needle and needles to the right.

*S*porting *faux pinecones and a jolly red bow, our Christmas Wreath Cake (above) makes a spectacular centerpiece. Winter Fruit Crisp (opposite) is a delightfully light concoction.*

CHRISTMAS WREATH CAKE

Pine Needles and Pinecones:
- 1 box (1 pound) confectioners' sugar
- 3 tablespoons meringue powder
- 1/2 teaspoon cream of tartar
- 6 to 8 tablespoons warm water
  Leaf green soft gel paste food color
- 3 teaspoons marzipan
- 1/4 cup sliced almonds

Cake:
- 2 1/4 cups cake flour (not self-rising)
- 1/3 cup unsweetened cocoa powder
- 2 teaspoons baking powder
- 1/2 teaspoon baking soda
- 1/2 teaspoon salt
- 3 ounces unsweetened chocolate, chopped
- 3/4 cup (1 1/2 sticks) butter, at room temperature
- 1 1/2 cups granulated sugar
- 3 eggs
- 1 teaspoon vanilla
- 1 1/4 cups milk

Italian Meringue:
- 2 cups granulated sugar
- 1/2 cup water
- 8 egg whites, at room temperature
- 2 teaspoons vanilla
- 1/8 teaspoon salt

Decorations:
- 1 tablespoon red-dot candies
- 1 strawberry fruit roll-up

1. Prepare Pine Needles and Pinecones: On low speed of an electric mixer, beat together confectioners' sugar, meringue powder, cream of tartar and warm water in small bowl until combined. Increase to high speed and beat for 10 minutes or until thick and glossy. Add food color paste for desired shade. Place plastic wrap directly on surface of icing until ready to use.

2. Line 3 large baking sheets with waxed paper. Fit medium-size pastry bag with coupler and plain writing tip. Fill with green icing. Pipe Pine Needle clusters in various sizes onto lined baking sheets (see

114

photos 1 and 2, opposite page). For each cluster, pipe 4 or 5 individual needles, about 1 inch long; pipe back and forth in 1 continuous motion without the tip leaving the waxed paper so each needle is a double thickness for added strength. Make more clusters of varying sizes with remaining icing. Let dry at room temperature for 5 hours or up to 1 day.

3. Shape 1 teaspoon of the marzipan into pinecone shape, about 1 inch long. Place sliced almonds, pointed side down and dark side up, overlapping, into one side of marzipan to form Pinecone. Cover with plastic wrap; set aside. Repeat with remaining marzipan and almonds.

4. Prepare Cake: Heat oven to 350°. Coat two 9 x 2-inch round cake pans with nonstick vegetable-oil cooking spray. Line bottoms of pans with waxed paper; coat paper with cooking spray.

5. Mix flour, cocoa powder, baking powder, baking soda and salt in bowl.

6. Melt chocolate in small saucepan over low heat; cool.

7. Beat together butter and sugar on medium-high speed in large bowl 2 to 3 minutes or until smooth and creamy. Add eggs, one at a time, beating well after each addition. Add vanilla and cooled chocolate; beat until combined. On low speed, beat in flour mixture alternately with milk in 3 additions, beginning and ending with flour; beat on medium speed for 2 to 3 minutes or until well blended. Evenly divide batter between 2 prepared pans.

8. Bake in 350° oven 30 to 35 minutes or until cakes spring back when gently touched on top and wooden pick inserted in centers comes out clean. Cool cakes in pans on wire rack for 10 minutes. Gently run knife around edge of cakes. Turn out onto wire rack to cool completely. If necessary, trim top of cakes with serrated knife so they are level.

9. Prepare Italian Meringue: Heat together sugar and water in small heavy-bottomed saucepan over medium-high heat until syrup registers 242° on candy thermometer, about 20 minutes; brush down sides of pan with wet pastry brush to prevent sugar crystals from forming.

10. Meanwhile, place egg whites in deep bowl in stand mixer fitted with a whisk attachment.

11. When syrup reaches 242°, remove from heat.

12. Beat egg whites on medium-high speed for about 15 seconds. Carefully pour hot syrup down sides of bowl into whites without hitting whisk (to avoid splattering hot syrup); beat 5 minutes on medium-high speed or until very thick.

13. Add the vanilla and salt; beat on high speed for 2 to 3 minutes or until glossy peaks form.

14. Decorate: Place small dollop of Italian Meringue in middle of cake plate to anchor cake. Place 1 cake layer on plate. Spread 1½ cups of Italian Meringue over the top of the cake. Place second layer on top. Use the remaining Italian Meringue to frost top and sides of cake.

15. Randomly place the Pinecones and the red-dot candies around the wreath.

16. With a small metal spatula, very gently pry the Pine Needles off the waxed paper. Arrange the needles in a random pattern around top edge of the cake to form a wreath. (The Pine Needles are very fragile and many will break as you place them on the cake; don't worry, since this actually will make the wreath look more authentic.)

17. Form a decorative bow with a strip of fruit roll-up and attach to the cake.
Yield: 16 servings.

WINTER FRUIT CRISP
Topping:
- 4 slices cinnamon-raisin bread, cubed
- ¼ cup (½ stick) unsalted butter, melted
- ½ cup sugar
- ½ teaspoon ground cloves
- 2 tablespoons sliced almonds

Fruit:
- 1 cup sugar
- 3 tablespoons all-purpose flour
- 3 large Golden Delicious apples (1½ pounds), peeled, cored and sliced
- 2 large pears (1 pound), peeled, cored and sliced
- 1½ cups fresh OR frozen and thawed cranberries
- 2 tablespoons lemon juice
  Vanilla ice cream (optional)

1. Heat oven to 375°.
2. Prepare Topping: Combine bread, butter, sugar, cloves and almonds in large bowl.
3. Prepare Fruit: Stir together sugar and flour in a large bowl until combined. Add apples, pears, cranberries and lemon juice, tossing until combined. Spoon into a 13 x 9 x 2-inch or oval baking dish. Sprinkle on topping, leaving 1-inch border of fruit showing around rim of dish. Tent loosely with aluminum foil. Place on baking sheet.
4. Bake in preheated 375° oven 1 hour 10 minutes or until bubbly and fruit in center of dish is tender when pierced with a fork. Remove foil during last 30 minutes of baking. Cool until warm. Serve with vanilla ice cream, if you wish.
Yield: 8 servings.

peace, joy, love
(pages 6-11)

GOLDEN PEARS

You need: Plastic pears; gold leaf kit; silky ribbons; gold braid; glue gun.

To do each: Apply gold leaf to pear following package directions. Tie silky ribbon in bow; glue to top. Loop a short piece of gold braid for hanger; glue at top of pear behind bow.

PAPER DOVE ORNAMENTS AND TREE TOPPER

You need: White textured paper; plain white paper (for backing); scissors; glue stick; glue gun and 3" of elastic (for topper only).

Cutting: Enlarge pattern (this page) as indicated for ornament and/or tree topper. Trace patterns for dove and separate wing on wrong side of textured paper and on plain paper. Flip patterns so some doves will face the other direction. Cut out.

Finishing: Glue backing dove and wing to wrong side of decorative paper dove and wing. Partially glue wing (up to lower scallops) to body (bottom edges even), bending top portion of wing outward to add dimension.

Topper only: Hot-glue ends of elastic to backing. Slip elastic over treetop.

LETTER ORNAMENTS

You need: Unfinished wooden letters (to form words – PEACE, JOY, LOVE); wood glue; red acrylic paint; paintbrush; gold leaf kit; gold cord.

To do: Paint letters red. When completely dry, glue letters together side-by-side to form words. When glue is set, apply gold leaf, following package directions. Tie ends of 8" cord length to each ornament for hanger.

SHEET-MUSIC ORNAMENTS

You need: Assorted sheet music; pie plate; brewed coffee or tea (for antiquing); $3^1/4$"W x $4^1/2$"L wooden rectangles; glue stick; drill with $^1/8$" bit; scissors; 12" of $^1/4$"W ribbon for each ornament; fishing line or nylon thread.

Preparing: Dip pieces of sheet music briefly in pie plate of coffee or tea to antique paper. Dry completely.

Cutting/decoupaging: Trace rectangle on wrong side of sheet music; cut out. Glue to wood.

Finishing: Drill a hole through center top edge of rectangle, from front to back, $^1/4$" down from top edge of ornament. Cut a piece of fishing line; thread through drilled hole; knot ends for hanger. Tie ribbon in bow; glue just below hole.

Paper Dove Ornaments
1 Square = 1"

Tree Topper
1 Square = 2"

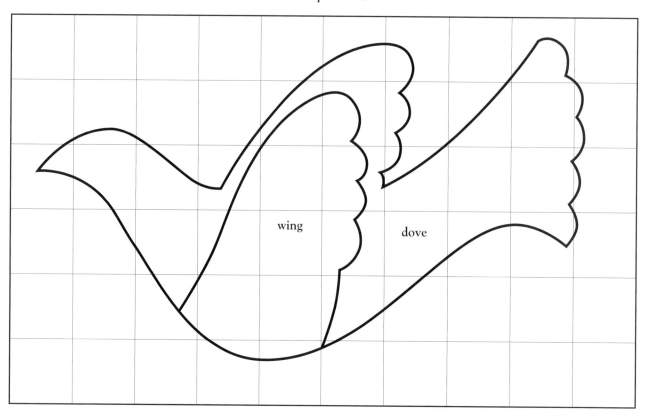

wing

dove

RED VELVET STOCKING

You need: Fabric – $5/8$ yd red velvet, $5/8$ yd coordinating lining; gold metallic sewing thread; 6"W x 16"L thin batting; $1/2$ yd gold-tasseled fringe trim; $1/2$ yd of $3/4$"W green velvet trim; $1/2$ yd of $1/4$"W gold braid trim; fabric glue; sewing supplies.

Cutting fabric: Enlarge pattern (this page); cut out. *Velvet* – Fold fabric in half; trace pattern. Cut out pair of stocking pieces. Unfold fabric. Cut a 6"W x 16"L cuff. Cut a 2"W x 7"L piece for hanging loop. *Lining* – Cut pair of stocking pieces same as for velvet.

Quilting cuff: Baste batting to wrong side of cuff piece. Thread sewing machine with gold metallic thread; machine-quilt cuff with random free-form swirls and spirals. Remove basting. Hem by gluing under long edges $1/2$".

Stitching stocking: *All stitching is done in $1/4$" seams, with right sides facing and raw edges even, unless noted.* Stitch stocking front to stocking back along side and lower edges, leaving upper edge open. Clip seams; turn. Stitch lining pieces together same as for velvet stocking. Do not turn. Press top edges of stocking and lining $1/4$" to wrong side. Slip lining inside stocking; slipstitch around top edge.

Adding cuff: Stitch short ends of cuff together to make tube. Slip cuff over top of stocking; slipstitch top edge of cuff to top edge of stocking.

Trimming cuff: Glue trims around bottom edge of cuff, starting with tasseled fringe (tassels hang below edge of cuff); glue velvet trim over lip of tasseled fringe (letting part of fringe lip show). Center and glue gold braid on top of velvet trim.

Adding hanging loop: Press under 7"L edges $1/4$", then fold in half lengthwise ($3/4$" x 7"); topstitch. Fold finished strip in half making a loop; hand-sew inside top/back edge of stocking.

GREEN VELVET BEADED STOCKING

You need: Fabric – $5/8$ yd olive-green velvet, $5/8$ yd coordinating lining; $1 1/2$ yds total of assorted ribbons (for diagonal cuff trim); fabric glue; two styles of beads – gold tone, red crystal; sewing supplies.

Cutting fabric: Enlarge pattern (this page); cut out. *Velvet* – Fold fabric in half; trace pattern. Cut out pair of stocking pieces. Unfold fabric. Cut a 6"W x 15"L cuff. Cut a 2"W x 7"L piece for hanging loop. *Lining* – Cut pair of stocking pieces same as for velvet. Cut a 6"W x 15"L cuff lining.

Beading stocking: On front piece, sew pairs (one gold, one red each) of beads randomly across stocking, except where they'll be hidden once cuff is added.

Stitching stocking: *All stitching is done in $1/4$" seams, with right sides facing and raw edges even, unless noted.* Stitch stocking front to stocking back along side and lower edges, leaving upper edge open. Clip seams; turn. Stitch lining pieces together same as for velvet stocking. Do not turn. Press top edges of stocking and lining $1/4$" to wrong side. Slip lining inside stocking; slipstitch around top edge.

Making cuff: *Cut ribbons only after positioning/pinning them on cuff.* Arrange/pin ribbons diagonally across cuff, spacing them $3/4$" apart. You may wish to layer some of the ribbons, placing narrow ones on top of wider ones. When pleased with arrangement, cut/unpin ribbons one at a time and glue in place. When glue is set, sew three pairs of beads (one gold, one red in each pair) along velvet between ribbons. Stitch cuff and cuff lining together along long edges; turn. Stitch short ends of cuff together to make tube; turn. Slip cuff over top of stocking; slipstitch top edge of cuff to top edge of stocking.

Adding hanging loop: Press under 7"L edges $1/4$", then fold in half lengthwise ($3/4$" x 7"); topstitch. Fold finished strip in half making a loop; hand-sew inside top/back edge of stocking.

Red Velvet Stocking and Green Velvet Beaded Stocking   1 Square = 1"

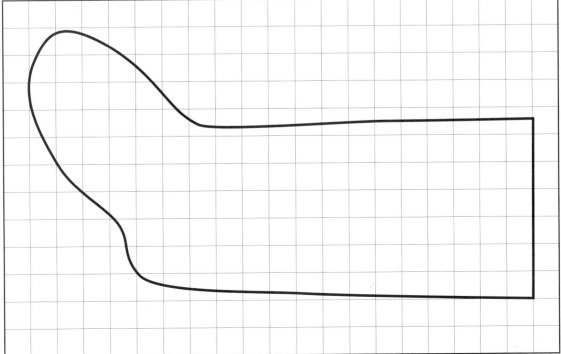

BOOT STOCKING

You need: Fabric – ⅝ yd plum velvet, ⅝ yd coordinating lining; 10" of ⅜"W plum satin ribbon; 1¾ yds of ¼"W gold trim; gold metallic thread; 10 gold shank buttons; four silk ribbon roses with leaves; sewing supplies.

Cutting fabric: Enlarge pattern (this page); cut out. *Velvet* – Fold fabric in half; trace pattern. Cut out pair of stocking pieces. *Lining* – Cut pair of stocking pieces same as for velvet.

Adding "laces": Fold gold trim in half and arrange/pin in crisscrossed "laces" up the toe-side edge of front velvet piece, folded end near toe and ends tied into a bow at top. Sew to velvet.

Stitching stocking: *All stitching is done in ¼" seams, with right sides facing and raw edges even, unless noted.* Fold plum ribbon (hanger) in half; pin to right side of one velvet piece at top/back edge, matching raw edges. Pin velvet piece to a lining piece at top edge only, right sides facing, hanger inside "sandwich." Stitch across top edge. Open out assembly and lay flat. Repeat with remaining velvet and lining pieces. Pin assemblies together, velvet to velvet, lining to lining; stitch all around, leaving opening in lining for turning. Turn right side out; slipstitch closed. Push lining inside stocking.

Finishing: Sew on pairs of buttons in center of top five "laces." Sew ribbon roses and leaves on right edge of top of stocking.

GREEN VELVET STOCKING WITH RUFFLED CUFF

You need: Fabric – ⅝ yd green velvet, ⅝ yd coordinating lining, ¼ yd cream-colored patterned silk shantung, ⅛ yd iridescent crinkly fabric; 7" of ¼" gold trim; ½ yd of 3"W gold braid; gold metallic thread; sewing supplies.

Cutting fabric: Enlarge pattern (this page); cut out. *Velvet* – Fold fabric in half; trace pattern. Cut out pair of stocking pieces. *Lining* – Cut pair of stocking pieces same as for velvet.

Embroidering velvet: Using gold thread and running stitches, embroider spirals and swirls randomly on front velvet piece, until spirals become an allover pattern. Do not embroider top portion of stocking that will be hidden once cuff is added.

Stitching: *All stitching is done in ¼" seams, with right sides facing and raw edges even, unless noted.* Stitch stocking front to stocking back along side and lower edges, leaving upper edge open. Clip seams; turn. Stitch lining pieces together same as for velvet stocking. Do not turn. Slip lining inside stocking. Set aside.

Making cuff: *Shantung* – Cut a 7"W x 15½"L strip. *Braid* – Center braid along length of shantung; stitch. Stitch short ends of cuff together to make tube. Do not turn. *Crinkly ruffle* – Cut a 3¼"W x 25"L strip. Hem one long edge ¼". Pin remaining long edge to bottom edge of cuff, gathering up fabric to fit; stitch.

Finishing: Fold gold trim into loop (hanger); slip inside lining (at top/back edge), loop facing downward, raw edges even; baste. Slip cuff inside lining (right side of cuff facing lining; loop inside "sandwich"), raw edges even. Stitch around the top edge. Pull out the cuff, and turn down over top edge of stocking.

Boot Stocking
1 Square = 1"

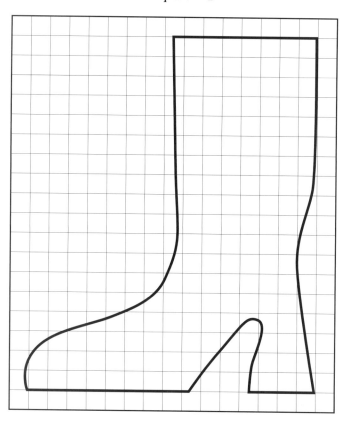

Green Velvet Stocking with Ruffled Cuff
1 Square = 1"

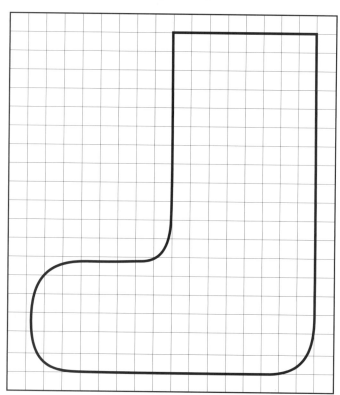

Fast & Festive:
counting the days
(pages 12-13)

TRIPTYCH CALENDAR

You need: 1" x 18" x 26" pine board; 4' of 1" x 8" pine; 18" x 24" piece of 1/4" plywood; 18" x 24" corrugated paper; decorative papers (2 yellow, 2 green); 3 1/2" wooden star; 24 mini wooden ornaments; gesso; acrylic paint (black, red, dark green, yellow, plus colors for ornaments); foam brushes; small paintbrush; sponge; letters/numbers cut from magazines; white glue; brass escutcheon pins; 5 upholstery tacks; 4 hinges; saber saw; drill w/bit; wire.

Making patterns: Enlarge patterns (page 120).

Cutting wood: *Pine* – Cut a center panel and two sides using patterns. *Plywood and corrugated paper* – Cut one tree each.

Painting: Prime and paint panels; see pattern and photo (page 12). *Checks* – Cut 1" and 1/2" squares from sponge; stamp 1" black checks on center panel and 1/2" black checks along side bottoms.

Making tree: Glue paper and wood trees together; paint as shown. Glue tree to center panel.

Decoupaging paper stars and holly: *Stars* – Trace; cut six large, seven small stars from yellow paper. *Holly* – Trace and cut 12 total leaves from green paper. Adhere motifs following photo. Tap a brass pin in center of each star.

Adding numbers, lettering: From magazines, cut numbers 1 to 24 and letters to spell "Merry Christmas." *Decoupaging* – Adhere lettering across holly leaves in center panel.

Numbers – On the left-side panel, adhere the numbers 1 to 12 to the left of X's on pattern. On the right-side panel, adhere numbers 13 to 24 as before.

Adding brass-nail pegs: Tap in pins at X's, leaving heads exposed 1/4".

Decorating wood star: Paint yellow. Cut a piece of yellow paper to fit center of star; adhere. Glue to top of center panel. Add tack at center.

Finishing: Add tacks along top edges. Join each side panel to center panel with two equally spaced hinges.

Painting ornaments: Paint as desired. Drill a tiny hole at top of each. Thread a short piece of wire through hole; twist wire into loop. Hang on pins tapped into tree and sides.

FABRIC GOODY BAGS

You need (for each of 24 bags): 4" x 12" print cotton fabric; 3"W x 3"H lightweight cardboard; 1/4 yd narrow trim; sewing supplies; dimensional fabric-paint writers; small treat or toy; 3/8 yd ribbon, rickrack or satin cord.

Making bag: Fold fabric crosswise, right sides together; stitch long edges with 1/4" seams. Turn. Fold under 1/4" on open edge of bag; stitch near fold to hem bag. Hand-stitch trim just below hem, turning under raw end of trim at bag seam.

Finishing: Place cardboard in bag. Using paint writer, write a date on center front of bag (number bags from 1 to 24), let dry. Remove cardboard. Place treat in bag. Tie ribbon, rickrack or cord around bag 1" from top.

FELT ENVELOPES

You need: Freezer paper; felt remnants in desired colors; pearl cotton in desired colors; paper-backed fusible web; muslin; rubber stamps with numbers; stamp pad with black fabric ink; embroidery needle; scissors; iron; pinking shears; assorted sequins; assorted glass rocaille beads; 24 small treats; double-sided tape (optional).

Cutting: Draw desired envelope shapes on freezer paper; cut out to make patterns. Set iron on warm; press patterns, shiny side down, onto felt. Cut a total of 24 assorted envelopes in same way, reusing patterns as needed. Peel off paper.

Stitching: Fold shapes into envelopes. Using contrasting pearl cotton and desired decorative stitches, stitch each envelope together.

Stamping: Following web manufacturer's directions, fuse web onto wrong side of muslin. Stamp numbers 1 through 24 onto right side of muslin; let dry. Cut out with pinking shears, leaving desired muslin border around each number; peel off paper backing. Fuse a number to each envelope.

Finishing: Stitch a sequin and bead on each corner of each number patch. For each hanging loop, knot ends of a 9" length of pearl cotton together; stitch knot to back of envelope. Place treat in each envelope. Secure flap of envelope, if desired, using double-sided tape.

ADVENT TREE

You need: Red and green tissue paper; 24 small gifts (chewing gum, pencils, memo pads, etc.); gold wire-edged ribbon; 24 manila hanging tags; rubber stamps with numbers; stamp pad.

To do: Wrap each gift in tissue paper; secure paper with ribbon bows. Stamp numbers 1 through 24 on tags. Tie a tag onto each gift. Tuck packages into the branches of your tree.

Triptych Calendar
1 Square = 1"

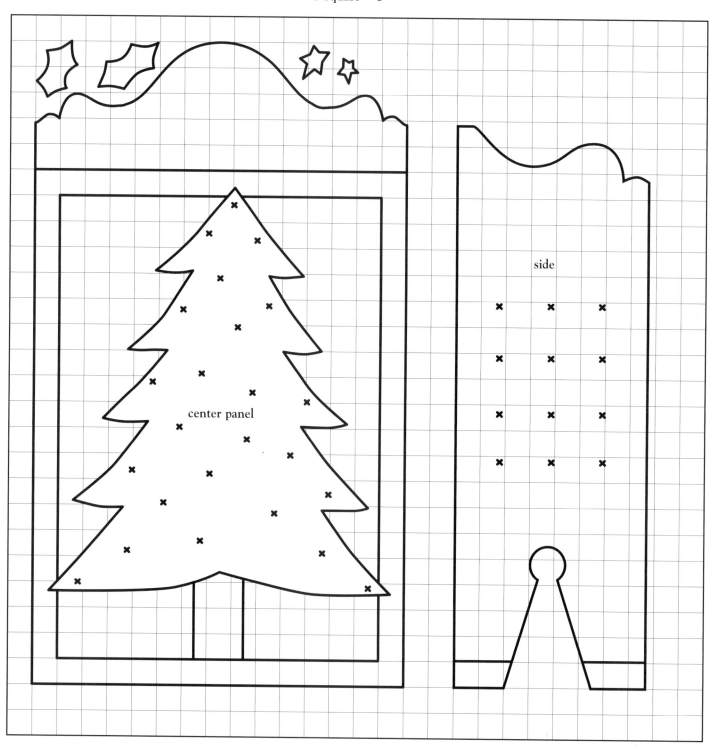

center panel

side

ADVENT CALENDAR CHAIR

You need: *Chair* – Pine (two 12' pieces of 2" x 2" for legs/post pieces, rungs; one 3' piece of 1" x 12" for tree, star; one 4' piece of 1" x 8" for aprons; one 15" x 15" piece of 1¼" board for seat); two 1¾" wood pyramids; 3½" piece of ⅜" dowel; wood glue; drywall screws; ⅜" wood plugs; sandpaper. ***Painting*** – Primer; transfer paper; tracing paper; acrylic paints (true red, yellow, light green, medium green, true green, true blue, deep blue, white, black, soft gray, blush, burnt umber, gold, deep mauve, medium orange, light orange); satin varnish; paintbrushes; sea sponge; ¼" and ⅜" checkerboard stencils. ***Trims*** – twenty-five 2" wooden gingerbread boy and girl figures; two 2" wooden stockings; mini artificial wreath; mini lights garland; 2 small jingle bells; cinnamon sticks; 25 small cup hooks; 33 upholstery tacks; thin wire; glue gun.

Cutting wood: *From 2" x 2"* – Cut two 39" pieces (back legs/posts); two 16" pieces (front legs); two 10½" pieces (front/back rungs); two 12⅞" pieces (side rungs). ***From 1" x 8"*** – Cut two front/back aprons 6½" x 10½"; two side aprons 6" x 12⅞"; cut notches as shown in diagrams. ***From 1" x 12"*** – Cut one 31" x 10½" piece (chair back); cut tree shape following diagram. Cut one 5½" x 6½" piece; sketch a star shape on piece and cut out.

Assembling: Drill pilot holes for screws. Assemble chair, following the diagrams. After assembly, conceal screw holes with wood plugs. Glue a pyramid "cap" on each chair post.

Painting: Prime wood; sand. Enlarge village pattern to fit side aprons; copy on aprons with transfer paper. Following the photo (page 13), paint chair as follows: ***Chair posts*** – Paint red. Mark off boot sections; paint boots black, fur trim white. Paint belt black, buckle gold. Copy face outlines; paint face blush; draw on eyes and mouth. Add white whiskers and hair. On sides, paint shading for arms, ending with a black mitten trimmed with white. Add white checks on hat with ¼" stencil. ***Back and front legs*** – Paint white. Add red checks with ⅜" stencil. ***Tree*** – Paint foliage true green and trunk burnt umber. Brush on branches with remaining greens, using "comma strokes." ***Seat*** – With sponges, paint base deep blue; shade edges with true blue. For Milky Way make a swirl stencil from tracing paper; spatter-paint white. In gold, add stars and "Merry Christmas to all…and to all a Good Night!" ***Village*** – Paint sky deep blue, windows yellow. Paint houses as desired. ***Window with curtains*** – Paint background deep blue, curtains thin wash of white. ***Mantel*** – Paint area white; brush on bricks in true red; shade with mauve. Sponge soft gray across entire section. ***Candy cane rungs*** – Paint white. Mask off 1¼" diagonal strips; paint, alternating red and white. When dry, add a green line on white stripes. Add white highlight line across red stripes. ***Star and dowel (not shown)*** – Paint star in checkerboard of medium and light orange. Paint dowel with narrow candy cane stripes same as above. Attach star to tree with dowel. ***Gingerbread people*** – Paint as shown in photo. Number 1 to 25 in black. ***Small wood stockings*** – Paint as desired. ***Verse*** – On sides and front of chair seat, with black paint write, " 'Twas the night before Christmas and all through the house, not a creature was stirring."

Trimming: Hot-glue cinnamon sticks on tree trunk. Hot-glue mini garland on village. Tap 25 upholstery tacks in chair-back calendar (to hang gingerbread numbers). Drill holes through gingerbread numbers and stockings; add wire loops. Insert cup hooks along underside of chair sides and rungs (to store numbers before hanging them on tree). Glue wreath on mantel. Tap in three tacks along sides of Santa's boots and on each mitten for hanging stockings. Attach a bell to each pyramid cap.

Note: Chair is for decorative use only.

Advent Calendar Chair – Side Aprons of Chair
Copy this outline to re-create the village shown on our chair – or create your own.
Paint a wooded forest, mountain scenery or Santa in his sleigh!

Advent Calendar Chair – Assembly Diagram

Here, we show the three views – front, side and top (seat) of our chair. For easy reference, enlarge these diagrams on a copier, and keep them close at hand while assembling your chair.

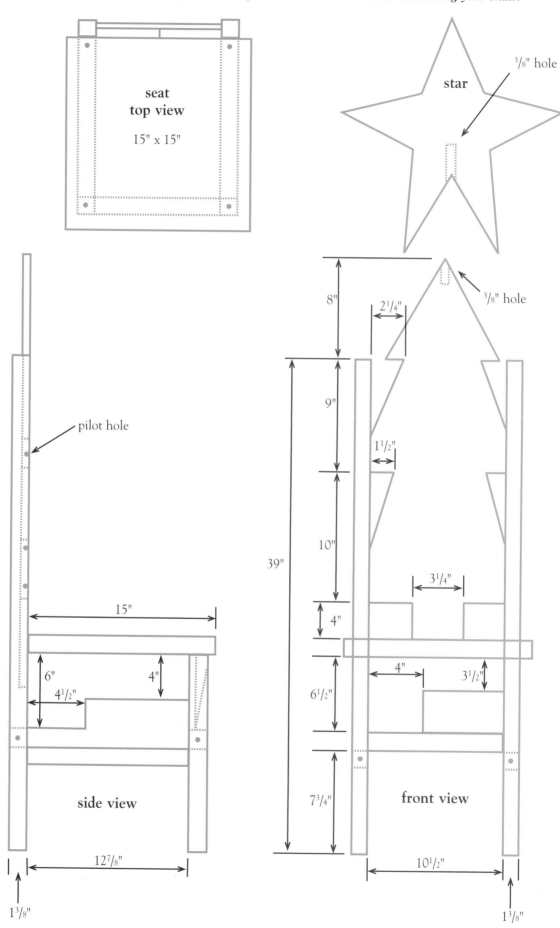

seat
top view

15" x 15"

star

3/8" hole

3/8" hole

8"

2¼"

9"

1½"

pilot hole

10"

39"

3¼"

15"

4"

6"

4"

4"

3½"

4½"

6½"

side view

front view

7¾"

12⅞"

10½"

1⅜"

1⅜"

royal treasures
(pages 14-19)

JESTER DOLL

You need: $^1/_2$ yd muslin; $^1/_2$ yd each of 4 colors of velvet; $^1/_4$ yd silk; fiberfill stuffing; doll-weighting pellets; fabric glue; 2 colored jingle bells; $^3/_8$ yd of $^1/_4$"W elastic; embroidery floss – blue, cranberry; cosmetic blush; sewing supplies.

Cutting: Enlarge patterns (page 124). Fold fabrics in half and cut through both layers to reverse pieces. From muslin, cut two head front sections, two head back sections, four arm sections and two body sections. From assorted colors of velvet, cut four leg sections, four hat sections, two shirt sections, two sleeves and two pants sections. From silk, cut one $6^1/_2$" x 50" collar.

Sewing: *All stitching is done in $^1/_4$" seams, with right sides facing and raw edges even, unless noted.* **Head** – Stitch head front sections together along front seam. Stitch back head sections together along back seam. Stitch head front to head back along sides. Clip curves; turn. Stuff firmly with mixture of fiberfill and pellets. **Body** – Stitch body sections together along sides, leaving upper and lower edges open; do not turn. **Legs** – Stitch each pair of leg sections together along side and lower edges, leaving upper edge open. Clip curves; turn. Stuff foot and ankle with pellets; stuff leg up to dotted line with fiberfill. Turn leg so seams meet in center; stitch along line. Stuff remainder of each leg with fiberfill. Baste open edge closed. "Sandwich" legs inside body, matching top edges of legs to lower edge of body. Baste legs (centered, 1" apart) to lower edge of body. Stitch body front and body back together along lower edge, catching tops of legs in seam. Turn body right side out. **Arms** – Stitch each pair of arm sections together along side and lower edges, leaving upper edge open. Clip curves; turn. Stuff hand portion of arm with pellets; stuff remainder of each arm with fiberfill. Turn under $^1/_4$" on upper edge of each arm; slipstitch openings closed. **Hat** – Stitch each pair of sections together along center seams to make hat front and back. Stitch hat front to back along sides and upper edges, leaving lower edge open. Turn under $^1/_4$" on lower edge; glue. Sew a bell to each point of hat. **Shirt** – Stitch shirt sections together along side seams. Turn under $^1/_4$" along upper edge. Sew running stitches along upper edge; do not cut thread. Turn under $^1/_2$" on lower edge; glue. **Sleeves** – Fold each sleeve in half; stitch underarm seams. Turn under $^1/_2$" on upper edge of each sleeve; slipstitch to shirt, just below neck. **Collar** – Fold collar in half lengthwise; stitch edges, leaving 5" opening along long side. Turn; slipstitch opening closed. Sew running stitches along one long edge. Pull up thread to gather collar to fit neck; secure gathers with several small stitches. **Pants—** Stitch pants sections together along center seam. Stitch inner leg seams. Turn under $^1/_2$" on waist edge; stitch near raw edge, leaving a 2" opening, to make casing. Insert elastic through casing; stitch ends together. Finish stitching casing closed. Turn under $^1/_2$" on each leg edge; glue.

Assembling: Stuff body firmly with fiberfill. Turn under $^1/_4$" on edges of upper opening. Insert lower edge of head into upper opening on body; pin. Glue, then stitch, head to body. Place shirt on body; pull up thread to gather to fit neck. Secure gathers with several small stitches. Glue collar around neck, with open ends in back. Slipstitch arms to shirt, inside sleeves.

Finishing: Embroider features on face. Apply blush to cheeks. Place pants on doll.

HARLEQUIN CHAIR

You need: Wood chair; 2 wood finials; two $1^1/_2$" lengths of dowel to fit hole in bottom of finials; drill with bit; wood glue; sandpaper; paintbrushes; wood primer; acrylic paints in desired colors; acrylic sealer.

Adding finials: Drill holes in top of chair where finials will be positioned. Apply glue to dowels. Secure finials to chair using dowels. Let glue dry completely.

Painting: Sand chair and finials. Paint with primer; let dry. Apply base color of paint to chair; let dry. Mark diamond pattern on flat surfaces of chair. Paint diamonds and finials assorted colors; let dry. Using contrasting color paint, outline diamonds, using "imperfect" lines; paint center of seat; let dry. Apply several coats of sealer to chair; let dry.

SILK TREE SKIRT

You need: $1^1/_2$ yds each of 3 colors of gold-printed raw silk; sewing supplies.

Cutting: From each fabric, cut one 49" x 17" panel.

Making skirt: Pin long edges of panels together, with right sides facing and raw edges even; place lightest color panel in center. Stitch panels in $^1/_2$" seams, forming square. Press seams toward darker fabrics. Fold square in quarters. Measure and mark curved line $24^1/_2$" from folded corner. Cut along line through all layers to make 49" circle. Make $24^1/_2$" long slash in center of center panel, from edge to center of circle for skirt opening. Turn under $^1/_4$", then $^1/_4$" again, on outer and opening edges. Press, easing in fullness around curves and mitering fabric at corners. Stitch close to folds to hem skirt and opening.

BRAIDED STAR AND BEADED BELL ORNAMENTS

You need: Wire star ornament form; metallic braid trim; glue gun; bell ornament form; prestrung molded bead strands; gold wire; beads.

Making star: Glue one end of braid to center of star. Glue and coil braid to cover center of star. Wrap braid around both sides of form to cover one point, gluing in same way. Trim braid end; glue in back. Wrap remaining points in same way.

Making bell: Glue one end of braid or doubled length of molded beads to top of bell, just below hanging loop. Wrap braid or beads around both sides of form to cover, gluing in same way. Glue braid trim around lower edges of bell outline.

Finishing each ornament: Cut 12" of wire for hanging loop. Fold wire in half; slip each end through wire at top of ornament and twist together to secure. String beads onto wire, pushing beads down to rest on ornament.

Jester Doll
1 Square = 1"

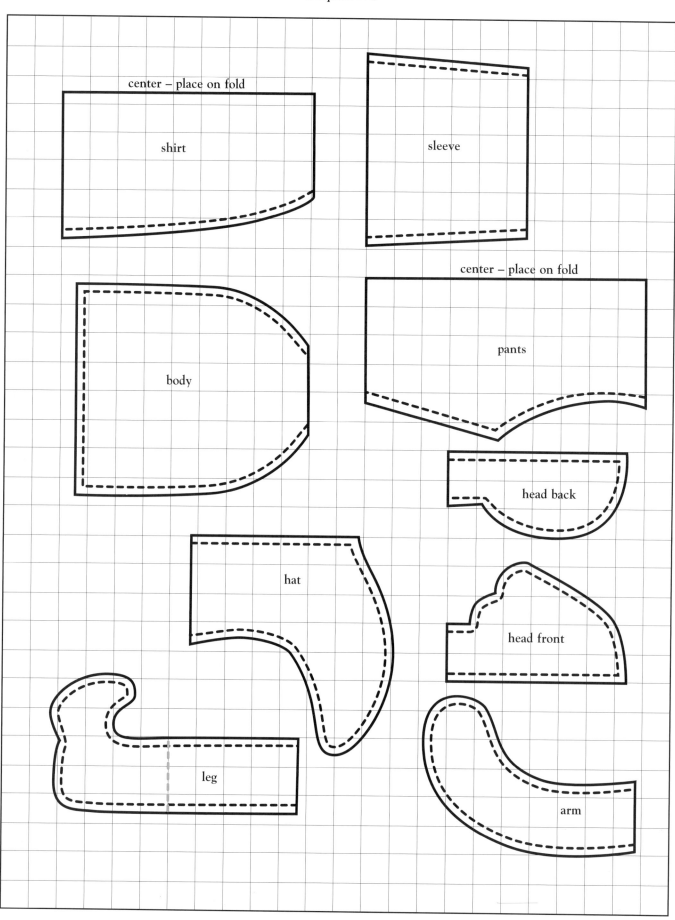

center – place on fold

shirt

sleeve

body

center – place on fold

pants

head back

hat

head front

leg

arm

VELVET CONES AND BALLS

You need: Assorted remnants of velvet, silk and sateen fabrics in coordinating colors; 4" and 6" plastic foam balls; 4¹/₂" and 6" plastic foam cones; assorted ¹/₄" gold metallic or coordinating trims; glue gun; scissors; pins; metallic-gold thread; assorted beads; tassels (optional).

Cutting: Measure around ball; cut enough pointed ovals from assorted fabrics to cover ball, cutting each piece on bias grain and allowing for slight overlaps of pieces. Measure and cut four triangles to cover side of each cone in same manner; cut additional circle to cover cone base.

Assembling: Place fabric pieces on foam pieces; secure edges with pins. (Edges will overlap.) Glue trim to cover each seam.

Finishing: Cut 12" of thread; knot ends together to make hanging loop. Glue, then pin, knot to top of ornament. Thread beads onto top of loop; knot thread above beads to secure. Glue tassel or bead to base if desired.

GILDED REINDEER

You need (for each): 6" square of ¹/₄" smooth plywood; transfer paper; scroll saw; sandpaper; metallic-gold spray paint; 12" of metallic cord.

Cutting: Enlarge pattern (this page). Transfer pattern to wood, with grain running from antlers to feet. Cut out; sand edges.

Painting: Apply several coats of spray paint, letting dry between coats.

Finishing: Tie cord ends around antlers to make hanging loop.

KING-SIZE CANDLESTICKS

You need: Clear pine or poplar pieces – four ¹/₄" x 6" x 36", two 2" x 2" x 36"; transfer paper; masking tape; scroll saw or jigsaw; sandpaper; 4 wood candle cups; wood glue; wood plaques – one 3" x 5", three 5" x 7"; acrylic gesso; assorted paintbrushes; metallic acrylic paints in desired colors; stencils in desired motifs; stencil adhesive; spray acrylic sealer.

Cutting: Enlarge patterns (page 126); transfer shapes onto two of the ¹/₄" boards. Tape one marked and one unmarked board together to cut mirror images; cut out. Sand. Measure from desired height of candle cup to base of each cutout; cut 2" x 2" to this measurement for each candlestick.

Assembling: Glue 2" x 2" to center of one cutout with bottom edges even. Glue matching cutout on back of 2" x 2" with bottom edges even. Glue bottom edges to center of desired plaque. Glue candle cup on top of 2" x 2" to make candlestick. Make each candlestick in same way.

Painting: Coat each candlestick with gesso; let dry. Sand. Apply two coats of desired metallic paint to entire candlestick.

Stenciling: Spray back of stencil with adhesive; press into position on candlestick. Stencil with desired color paint. Remove stencil; let dry.

Finishing: Spray with several coats of sealer, letting dry between coats.

Gilded Reindeer
1 Square = 1"

King-Size Candlesticks
1 Square = 1"

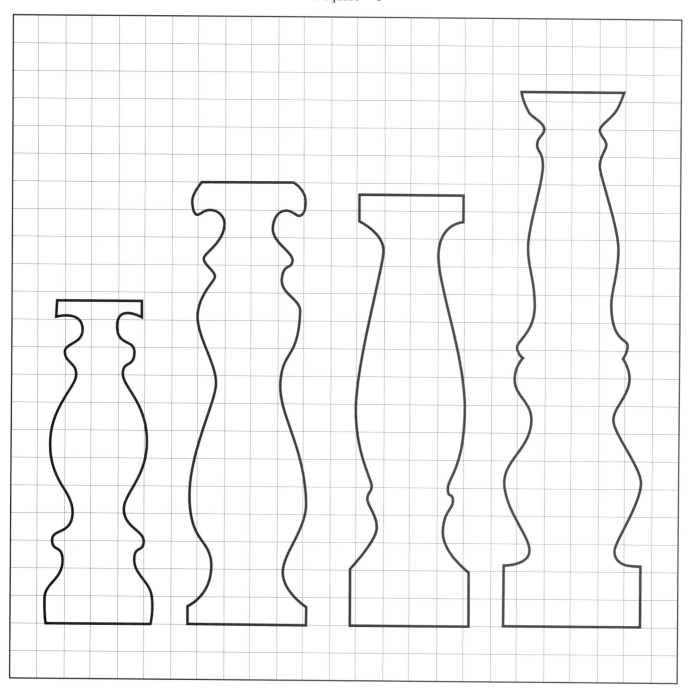

ORGANZA MANTEL SCARF

You need: Organza fabrics – 2 yds each in gold print and purple solid; sewing supplies.

Cutting: From each fabric, cut one 66" x 16" panel. Mark center of each short end. Mark each long side 4" from each short end. Connect marks at each short end to form point; cut along marked lines.

Sewing: Sew panels together, with right sides facing and raw edges even. Use a $^1/_2$" seam, leaving 6" opening along one long side. Trim corners; turn. Press. Slipstitch opening closed.

RIBBON SOCK

You need: $^1/_2$ yd muslin fabric; fusible web; 3 yds each of two $1^7/_8$"W satin ribbons; $^1/_2$ yd lining fabric; $^3/_4$ yd gold braid trim; 1 yd narrow wire-edged ribbon; sequins; sewing supplies.

Weaving ribbon: Cut two 16" x 14" pieces from muslin and two corresponding pieces from web. Follow manufacturer's directions to fuse web to muslin pieces. Remove paper backing. Cut satin ribbon into lengths equal to width and length of muslin. Place muslin pieces web side up. Arrange ribbon in rows across width of each base, alternating colors and leaving very narrow space between ribbons. Pin ribbon ends to edges of base. Weave remaining ribbons in and out of pinned ribbons and pin ends in same way. Follow manufacturer's directions to fuse ribbons to base.

Cutting: Enlarge pattern (page 128). From one woven-ribbon piece, cut stocking front. Flip pattern over to cut stocking back from remaining woven-ribbon piece. Cut lining front and back in same manner.

Assembling: *All stitching is done in $^1/_4$" seams, with right sides facing and raw edges even, unless noted.* Stitch stocking front to lining front along top edge; open out flat. Stitch stocking back to lining back in same manner. Place pieces together, matching stocking front to stocking back and lining front to lining back. Stitch along all edges, leaving an opening in lining. Clip curves; turn. Slipstitch opening closed. Push lining down into stocking.

Finishing: Hand-stitch braid to top edge of stocking, leaving a $2^1/_2$" loop at upper back corner for hanging loop. Hand-stitch wire-edged ribbon to stocking, arranging ribbon in free-form shapes as you stitch. Hand-stitch sequins over ribbon as desired.

HIGH-HEELED SILK STOCKING

You need: Printed raw silk fabrics – $^1/_2$ yd for stocking, $^1/_4$ yd for cuff; 1 yd gold braid trim; sewing supplies.

Cutting: Enlarge pattern (page 129). Fold stocking fabric in half; trace stocking pattern, including heel. Cut stocking front and back. Fold cuff fabric in half; trace heel pattern. Cut two heel sections. Unfold; cut one 7" x 11" cuff.

Assembling: *All stitching is done in $^1/_4$" seams, with right sides facing and raw edges even, unless noted.* Make $^1/_8$" clips along inner curved edge of each heel section, spacing clips about $^1/_4$" apart. Turn under $^1/_4$" on clipped edge; press. Pin a heel to each stocking section, with right sides up and raw edges even. Baste raw edges together. Hand-stitch along fold to attach each heel to each stocking section. Stitch stocking front to stocking back along side and lower edges, leaving upper edge open. Clip

seams; turn. Press. Fold cuff in half crosswise; stitch short edges together to make tube. Place stocking inside cuff. Stitch one edge of cuff to upper edge of stocking, seams aligned. Turn under $^1/_4$" on remaining edge of cuff for hem; pin to inside upper edge of stocking, over seam. Hand-stitch hem to stocking.

Finishing: Starting at back edge, hand-stitch trim to bottom edge of cuff, forming curls at center front and center back. Hand-stitch trim to top edge of cuff, forming a $2^1/_2$" loop in trim at upper back corner to form hanging loop.

JESTER BOOT

You need: $^1/_2$ yd red velvet for stocking; $^1/_4$ yd printed raw silk for cuff; $^1/_4$ yd fabric for cuff lining; $^3/_4$ yd gold braid trim; gold tassels; sewing supplies.

Cutting: Enlarge patterns (page 130). Fold red velvet in half; trace stocking pattern. Cut stocking front and back. From raw silk, cut one cuff. From lining fabric, cut one cuff lining.

Assembling: *All stitching is done in $^1/_4$" seams, with right sides facing and raw edges even, unless noted.* Stitch stocking front to stocking back along side and lower edges, leaving upper edge open. Clip seams; turn. Fold cuff in half crosswise; stitch short ends together to make tube. Make tube from cuff lining in same way. Stitch cuff to lining along pointed edges. Trim seams; turn. Press. Turn under $^1/_4$" on remaining raw edge of cuff only; press. Slip stocking inside cuff. Stitch lining only to upper edge of stocking, seams aligned, keeping cuff free. Pin fold of cuff to inside upper edge of stocking, over seam. Hand-stitch folded edge to stocking.

Finishing: Starting at back edge, hand-stitch trim to cuff, forming curl at center front and center back. At upper back corner, form $2^1/_2$" loop in trim; stitch end to cuff to form hanging loop. Hand-stitch tassel to tip of each cuff point.

VELVET ELF BOOTIE

You need: Velvet – $^1/_2$ yd purple for stocking, $^1/_2$ yd gold for cuff; $^1/_2$ yd purple organza fabric; $^1/_2$ yd beaded braid trim; sewing supplies.

Cutting: Enlarge pattern (page 131). Fold purple velvet in half; trace stocking pattern. Cut stocking front and back. From organza, cut two pieces for overlay front and back in same manner. From gold velvet, cut one 10" x $11^1/_2$" cuff.

Assembling: *All stitching is done in $^1/_4$" seams, with right sides facing and raw edges even, unless noted.* Baste each overlay to each corresponding stocking section, right sides up. Working with both layers together, stitch stocking front to stocking back along side and lower edges, leaving upper edge open. Clip seams; turn. Fold cuff in half crosswise; stitch short ends together to make tube. Place stocking inside cuff. Stitch one edge of tube to upper edge of stocking, seams aligned. Turn under $^1/_4$" on remaining edge of tube for hem; pin to inside upper edge of stocking, over seam. Hand-stitch hem to stocking.

Finishing: Hand-stitch trim to lower edges of cuff. Cut 6" of trim for hanging loop; stitch ends together. Stitch ends inside upper back corner of stocking.

Ribbon Sock
1 Square = 1"

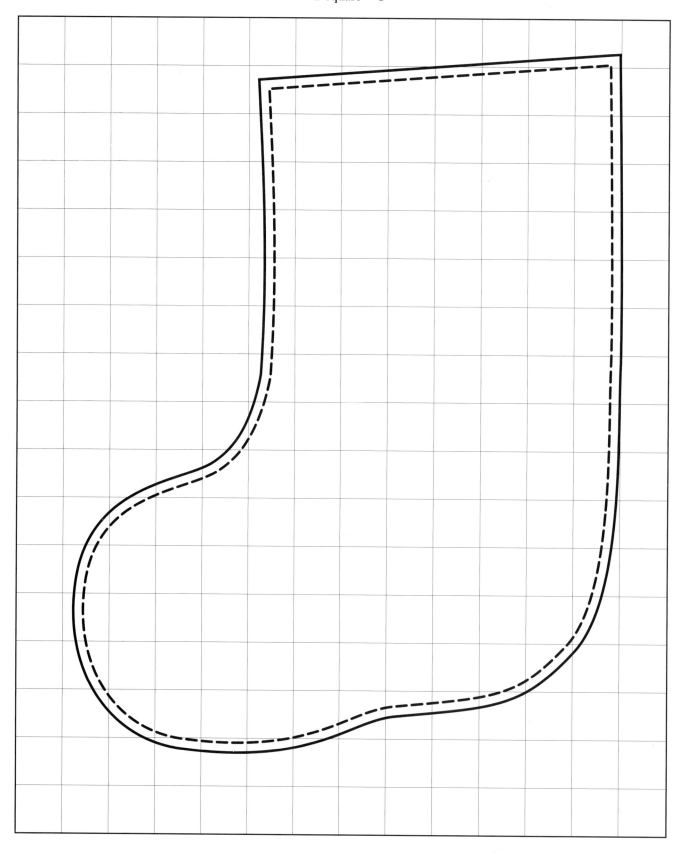

High-Heeled Silk Stocking
1 Square = 1"

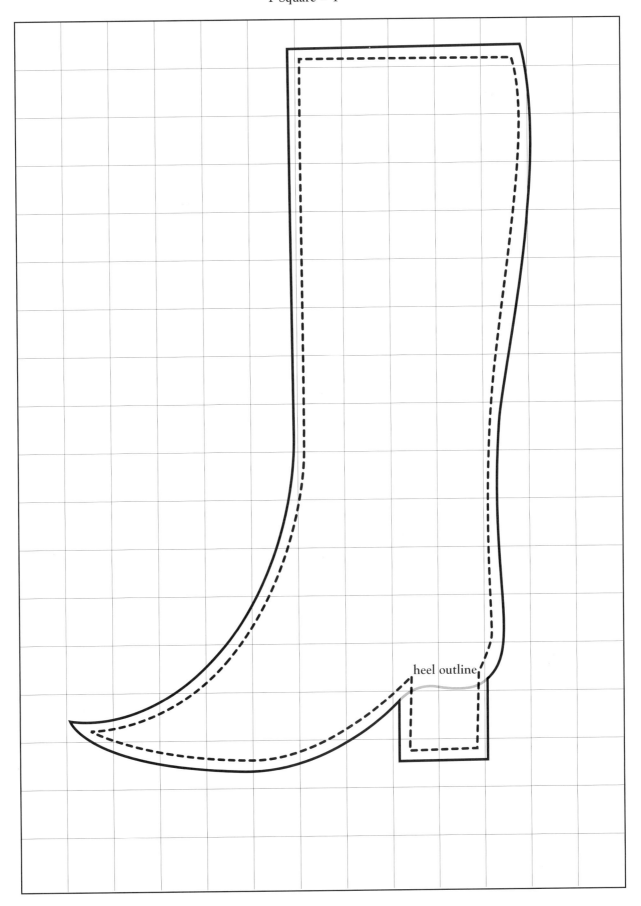

heel outline

Jester Boot
1 Square = 1"

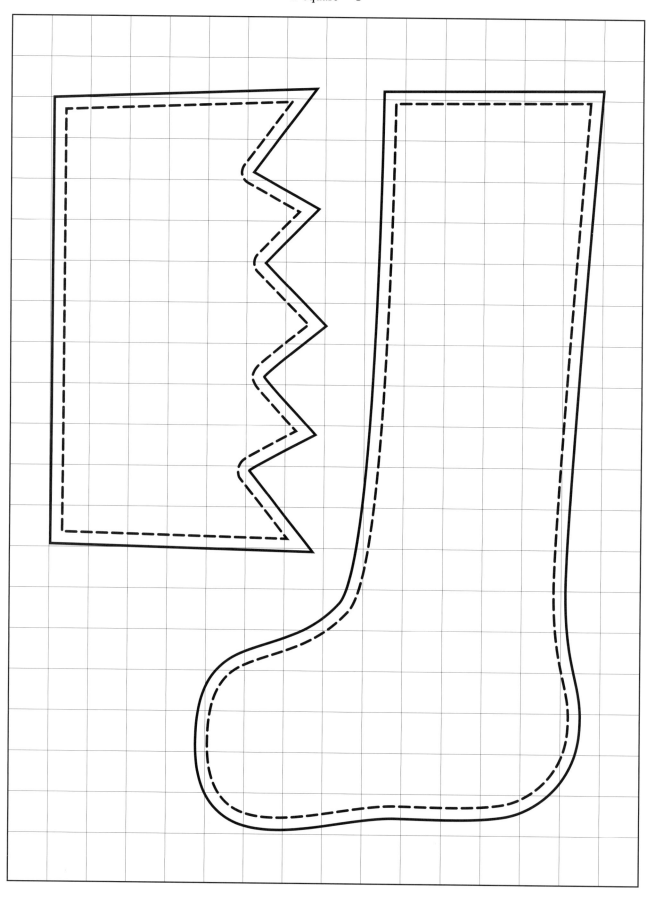

Velvet Elf Bootie
1 Square = 1"

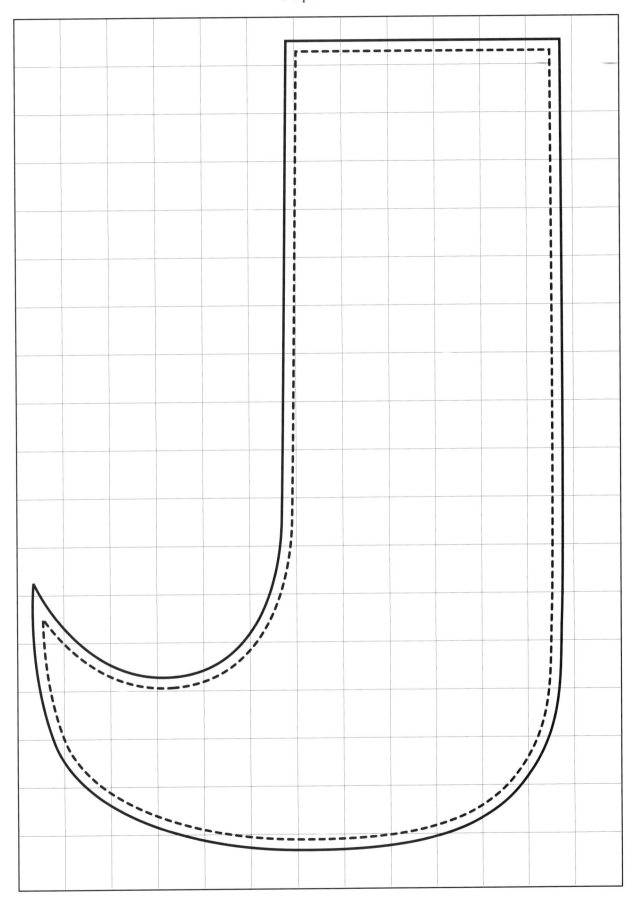

shimmer and shine
(pages 20-25)

BERIBBONED SILK STOCKING

You need: $1/2$ yd silk fabric; sheer ribbons in desired colors; sewing supplies.

Cutting: Enlarge pattern (page 133). Fold fabric in half; cut two pieces for stocking front and back.

Sewing: *All stitching is done in $1/4$" seams, with right sides facing and raw edges even, unless noted.* Stitch stocking front to back, leaving upper edge open. Clip curves, turn. Turn under $1/4$", then $1/4$" again on upper edge; stitch close to fold to hem. To make hanging loop, cut 8" of ribbon; fold in half. Hand-stitch ends to upper back corner of stocking.

Making ribbon fringe: Cut one ribbon piece 2" longer than upper edge of stocking to use for fringe base. Cut remaining ribbons into assorted lengths. Tie ribbons onto base to make fringe. Hand-stitch fringe to upper edge of stocking.

HIGH-HEELED VINYL BOOT

You need: $1/2$ yd vinyl fabric; rhinestone buttons; sewing supplies.

Cutting: Enlarge pattern (page 133). Fold vinyl in half; cut two pieces for stocking front and back.

Sewing: *All stitching is done in $1/4$" seams, with right sides facing and raw edges even, unless noted.* Stitch stocking front to back, leaving upper edge open. Clip curves, turn. Turn under $1/4$", then $1/4$" again on upper edge; stitch close to fold to hem.

Finishing: Cut a 6" x 1" piece of vinyl; fold in half to form hanging loop. Hand-stitch loop to upper back corner of stocking. Sew buttons to boot as desired.

SLANT-CUFF SATIN STOCKING

You need: $1/2$ yd satin for stocking; $1/4$ yd satin for cuff; sewing supplies.

Cutting: Enlarge pattern (page 134). Trace stocking and cuff patterns separately. Fold fabrics in half. From larger fabric, cut two pieces for stocking front and back. From smaller fabric, cut four pieces for cuff and cuff lining.

Sewing: *All stitching is done in $1/4$" seams, with right sides facing and raw edges even, unless noted.* Stitch stocking front to back, leaving upper edge open. Clip curves, turn. Stitch two cuff sections together along each side edge to make a loop. Stitch cuff lining in same way. Insert cuff in lining, with seams aligned; stitch lower edge. Turn. Place cuff inside stocking so right side of cuff faces wrong side of stocking. Stitch upper edge; turn cuff to right side.

Finishing: Cut a 6" x 2" piece of fabric. Fold in half lengthwise; stitch long edge to form hanging loop. Turn; hand-stitch loop to upper back corner of stocking.

FEATHERED SHANTUNG SOCK

You need: $1/2$ yd shantung fabric; wide feather trim; sewing supplies.

Cutting: Enlarge pattern (page 135). Fold fabric in half; cut two pieces for stocking front and back.

Sewing: *All stitching is done in $1/2$" seams, with right sides facing and raw edges even, unless noted.* Stitch stocking front to back, leaving upper edge open. Clip curves, turn. Turn under $1/4$", then $1/4$" again, on upper edge; stitch close to fold to hem.

Finishing: Cut a 6" x 2" piece of fabric. Fold in half lengthwise; stitch long edge to form hanging loop. Turn; hand-stitch loop to upper back corner of stocking. Slipstitch feather trim to upper edge of stocking.

CHRISTMAS TREE SCARF

You need: $5^1/2$ yds of 54"W lightweight fabric; sheer ribbons in assorted colors and widths; sewing supplies.

Cutting and sewing: Cut two 8' x 4' pieces of fabric. Pin pieces together with right sides facing. Stitch edges in $1/4$" seams, leaving opening along one side; turn. Slipstitch opening closed.

Making ribbon fringe: Cut two 8' and two 4' lengths of ribbon for fringe base. Cut remaining ribbons into assorted lengths. Tie ribbons onto base pieces to make fringe. Hand-stitch fringe to skirt.

STARDUST ORNAMENTS

You need: Extra-large white pom-poms; assorted ribbons; low-temp glue gun; scissors.

To do each: Cut an 8" ribbon length for hanging loop. Glue ends to center of pom-pom. Fluff pom-pom.

SHANTUNG NAPKINS AND SILK TABLE SKIRT

You need: Silk shantung fabric; chalk pencil; 2"W beaded fringe; sewing supplies.

Measuring: Measure width of table. Measure height of table from top to floor; subtract $1^1/2$" for drop. Add twice drop measurement to width to determine finished cutting size of skirt.

Cutting: Cut square of fabric, using cutting size for each side, piecing if needed. Fold fabric into quarters. Divide cutting measurement in half. Starting at folded corner, measure and mark curve along outer edge of fabric, using this measurement. Cut through all layers. Cut 19" square of fabric for each napkin.

Finishing: Press skirt and napkin edges under $1/4$", then $1/4$" again, folding in fullness at napkin corners. Pin lip of fringe under pressed edge of skirt; stitch close to pressed edge. Stitch close to pressed edges of napkins. Cut two or three bead sections from fringe for one corner of each napkin. Hand-stitch fringe to napkins.

Beribboned Silk Stocking
1 Square = 1"

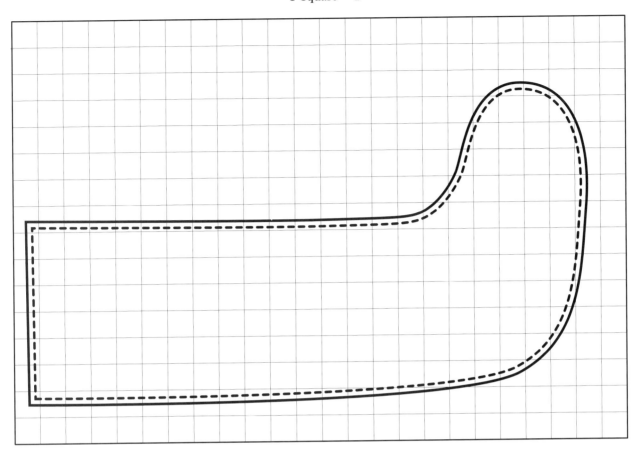

High-Heeled Vinyl Boot
1 Square = 1"

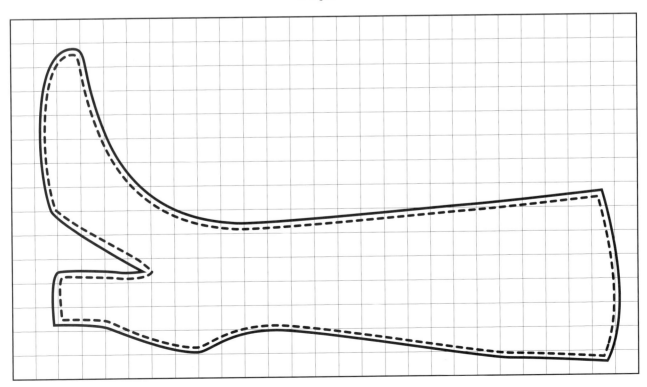

133

Slant-Cuff Satin Stocking
1 Square = 1"

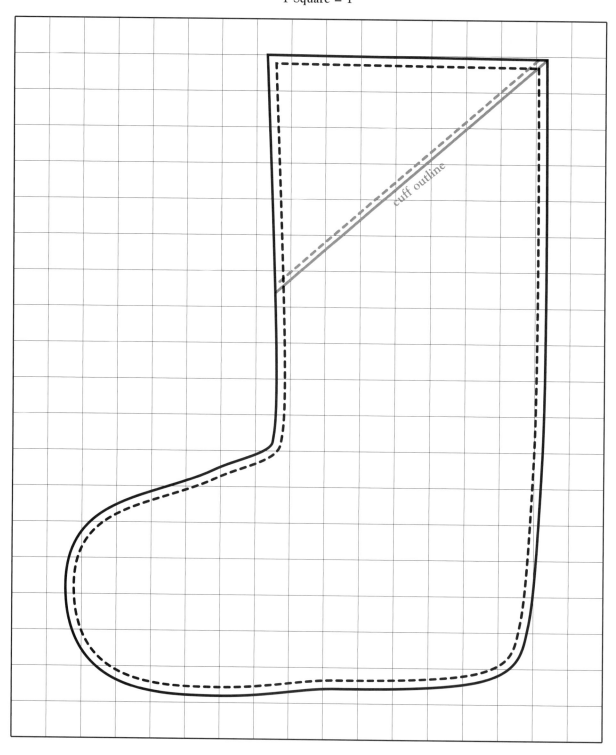

cuff outline

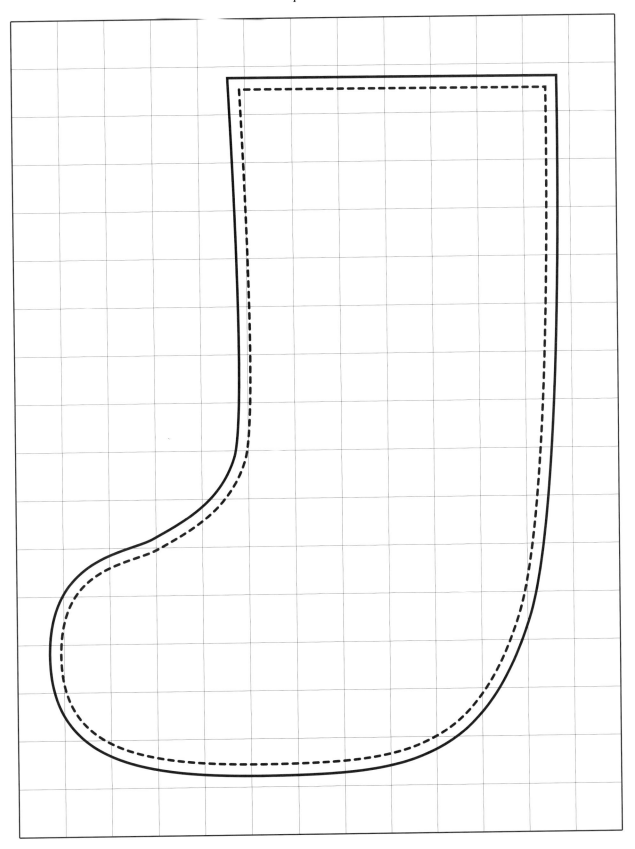

CRUSHED-VELVET BEAR

You need: 1¼ yds crushed velvet; fiberfill stuffing; silver embroidery thread; chalk pencil; awl; 5 snap-on doll joints; heavy-duty thread; 2 silver buttons; ¾ yd wire-edged ribbon; sewing supplies.

Cutting: Enlarge patterns (page 137). Fold velvet in half; cut four ear sections, two head sides, one gusset, two body front sections, two body back sections, four arm sections, four leg sections and two paws. Transfer marks to wrong side of each piece.

Sewing: *All stitching is done in ½" seams, with right sides facing and raw edges even, unless noted.* **Head** – Stitch each pair of ear sections together along curved edges, leaving straight edge open. Clip curves; turn. Stuff lightly; baste closed. Stitch an ear to dart on each head side. Fold each head side, matching dart markings; stitch darts. Stitch gusset to one head side, matching marks. Stitch gusset to remaining head side. Trim seams; turn. Stuff firmly. **Arms** – Stitch each pair of arm sections together, leaving opening along back edge. Trim seams; turn. Stuff paw area. **Legs** – Stitch each pair of leg sections together along side edges, leaving lower edges open. Also leave opening in center back. Stitch a paw to lower edge of each leg. Trim seams; turn. Stuff foot area. **Body** – Stitch body front sections at center front seam. Stitch body back sections together at center back seam, leaving 4" opening. Stitch body front to body back, leaving ¼" opening at neck. Trim seams; turn right side out.

Assembling: Using awl, poke holes at arm and leg marks. Follow joint manufacturer's directions to attach joints at marks. Using heavy-duty thread, sew running stitches along neck edge of head. Pull up thread to gather neck edge tightly around remaining joint; knot thread ends to secure. Insert other end of joint into neck opening on body; slipstitch opening closed around joint. Stuff body firmly; slipstitch opening closed. Finish stuffing arms and legs; slipstitch openings closed.

Finishing: Using silver thread, embroider nose and mouth. Sew on buttons for eyes. Tie ribbon around bear's neck.

meringue magic (page 87)

Meringue Poinsettias

Crushed-Velvet Bear
1 Square = 1"

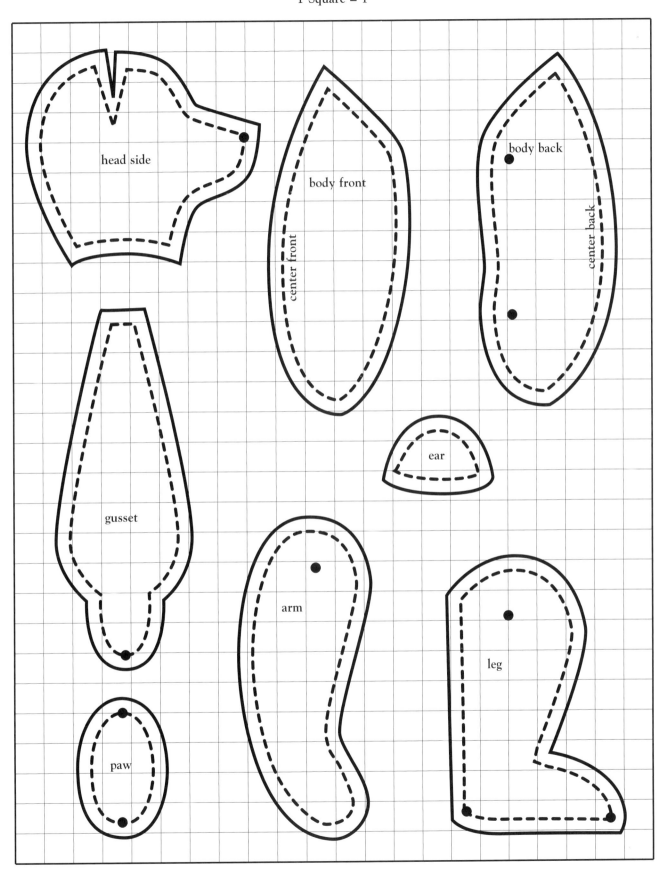

Fast & Festive:
here, there & everywhere
(pages 26-27)

GOODY-FILLED PAPER CONE
You need: White watercolor paper; stiff paper in green and red; embroidery thread; needle; snowflake rubber stamp; white ink stamp pad; scissors; decorative-edged scissors; craft glue; glitter pen; glue-on rhinestones; small paillette sew-on trim; ribbon.
Assembling: From white paper, cut two triangles, each approximately 8"W x 11"H, for cone. Holding cone pieces together, use embroidery thread and whipstitch around two long edges to close. Keep stitches about $1/4$" apart and leave top short edge open. Use snowflake stamp and white ink to stamp snowflakes on green paper. Cut out around edges of snowflakes. Glue snowflakes on cone randomly, trimming away excess as necessary at side edges. Decorate snowflakes with glitter pen and rhinestones. Cut a length of green paper to fit across top open edge and glue in place. Cut narrow strips of red paper with decorative-edged scissors. Cut and fit narrow strips crisscrossed along green top border and glue in place. Decorate with glitter pen. Cut small pieces of red and green paper to fit on tip of cone and glue in place. Cut a length of paillette trim to fit along bottom edge of green border and glue in place. Cut a 12" length of ribbon for hanger. Glue ends inside cone.

BOWL OF CANDLES
You need: Sand; coarse glitter; star confetti; large, deep bowl; taper candles.
To do: Mix sand, glitter and confetti in bowl to a depth of 2" or more. Insert candles into sand at varying angles.
Note: Never leave burning candles unattended.

ELEGANT STEMWARE TASSELS
You need: Assorted narrow ribbons; thin gold yarn; cardboard; scissors.
Assembling: Cut a rectangle from cardboard, desired tassel length x about 4"W. Wrap ribbons lengthwise around cardboard piece until tassel is desired thickness. Begin and end ribbon pieces along bottom edge. Tie a length of yarn around ribbon pieces at top edge and knot securely, leaving a long tail for attaching. Cut ribbons apart at bottom edge. Wrap another yarn length around tassel about $3/4$" from knotted end and knot securely. Tuck ends into tassel to hide.

STARRY NAPKIN RING
You need: Star cookie cutter; 22-gauge wire; wire cutters; beads.
To do: Bend wire around cookie cutter to determine length of wire needed. Cut wire slightly longer. String beads onto wire. Twist wire ends together to secure. Reshape wire if needed.

FAUX-ETCHED MIRROR
You need: Mirror; ivy stencil; spray-on snow; low-tack painter's tape; silk roses; wire-edged ribbon; floral wire; scissors.
"Etching" mirror: Tape stencil to mirror. Lightly spray snow over stencil; remove stencil. Repeat as desired. Be careful not to touch stenciled areas.
Finishing: Tie ribbon in a bow. Wire bow and roses together. Wire arrangement to top of mirror.

FESTIVE CHANDELIER
You need: Chandelier; fresh greenery and mistletoe; floral wire; wire-edged ribbon; scissors.
To do: Weave trailing vines of greenery around chandelier hardware; wire in place as needed. Gather sprigs of mistletoe under base of each light; wire in place. Tie ribbon bows to chandelier.

holiday in white
(pages 28-33)

EMBROIDERED STAR AND DOVE
You need: White felt; cookie cutter or other template in dove or star; #5 pearl cotton embroidery thread – white, blue, green, gold metallic; #8 pearl cotton embroidery thread – white; 2.5mm white pearl beads; 3.5mm white pearl beads; gold faceted cup sequins; beading needle; metallic ribbon; wired edged ribbons; sewing supplies; fiberfill stuffing.
Cutting: Fold felt in half. Using template, outline motif. Cut through both layers to cut out front and back pieces.
Embroidery: *Follow embroidery diagrams (page 156) and work embroidery from center out towards edges. Star* – Following photo (page 28), sew a sequin and bead in center. Work a row of French knots around center bead, then a row of beads around knots. From center to points, work chain stitch or lazy daisy stitches and sew on sequins and pearls around center as desired. Whipstitch around chain stitch with gold thread. *Dove* – Following photo (page 31), chain stitch wing and breast of dove about $1/2$" from edge with colored thread. Whipstitch around threads of chain stitch with gold thread. Work lazy daisy stitches with gold thread to make tail feathers. Fill in spaces with French knots in colored thread and pearl beads. Use thinner white thread to sew on beads. Position a sequin under larger beads and sew them on together for eye and interspersed around dove. Sew French knots in colored thread and pearls along edge of head and breast, alternating placement. Work chain stitch in gold for beak. Sew beads on inside edge of beak. Fill in spaces with beads.
Finishing: Cut a 10" length of ribbon for hanging loop. Fold in half crosswise and sandwich raw edges at top between front and back piece. With wrong sides facing, sew front and back together with thinner white thread and chain stitch. Stuff star or dove firmly with fiberfill before closing completely. Tie wire-edged ribbons into bows around hanger as desired.

STARRY WHITE TABLECLOTH

Size: 74" square

You need: 4½ yds white organza; 12 yds of ⅞"W white, double-sided satin ribbon; white felt; fusible web; 8mm clear sequins; sewing supplies.

Cutting/stitching: *When sewing, match right sides and raw edges and use a ½" seam, unless noted.* Cut four 38" x 38" squares from organza. Stitch two squares together along one side. Stitch remaining two squares together in same manner. Sew assemblies together along one long edge, forming a large square. Press raw edges under ½".

Adding trim: Spread out cloth, right side up. Pin ribbon to cover seams; stitch. Pin ribbon around edges; stitch.

Making stars: Enlarge star pattern (this page) to make three sizes – 4"W, 6"W, and 8"W. Trace desired number of stars on paper backing of web. Follow web manufacturer's directions to fuse web to felt. Cut out stars. Position stars randomly on tablecloth; fuse. Sew sequins to stars.

Starry White Tablecloth Star
Enlarge to 4"W, 6"W and 8"W

SUGARED FRUIT

You need: Fresh, firm fruit (apples, grapes and plums work well); pasteurized or reconstituted egg whites; superfine sugar; waxed paper; wire racks.

To do: Lightly whisk egg whites in a small bowl. Dip fruit with a fork, letting excess drip back into the bowl. Set on waxed paper. Drop fruit in a shallow dish filled with superfine sugar; use a spoon to sprinkle more sugar on top. Gently remove to a wire rack and allow to dry until firm and egg white is no longer tacky to touch.

CHIFFON TREE SKIRT

Note: Tree skirt consists of a large bordered square (48") topped by a small bordered square (36").

You need: 42"W chiffon fabric – 3⅞ yds white, 3½ yds blue; sewing supplies.

Cutting fabric for large square: *White* – Cut one 41" x 41" square (skirt) and one 10" x 10" square (facing). Cut a 5"-dia hole in center of facing. Cut two 2"W x 54"L bias strips (ties), pieced as needed. *Blue* – Cut eight 5"W x 51"L strips (border), following lengthwise grain of fabric.

Cutting fabric for small square: *Blue* – Cut one 31" x 31" square (skirt) and one 10" x 10" square (facing). Cut a 5"-dia hole in center of facing. Cut two 2"W x 45"L bias strips (ties), pieced as needed. *White* – Cut eight 4"W x 39"L strips (border), following lengthwise grain of fabric.

Stitching facing to each skirt square: With right sides facing and corners aligned, pin facing to center of skirt square. Stitch ½" from circle opening. Following cut edge, trim ½" from stitching, cutting a hole in center of skirt. Clip seam allowance every ½" up to the stitching line. Turn facing to wrong side of skirt; press. Press under ½" on each straight edge of facing; topstitch to skirt.

Adding border to each skirt: With right sides facing, long edges even, center one border strip on one edge of skirt. Use a ½" seam and sew border to skirt, leaving ½" unstitched at each end. Repeat with remaining border strips. At each corner, press and pin each pair of border ends to create a diagonal (mitered) corner. Stitch along pressing lines. Trim excess fabric, leaving a ½" seam allowance. Press mitered seam open. Press borders flat.

Finishing border: Press under ½" on raw edge of skirt border. Fold each border in half to wrong side of skirt, matching pressed edge to stitching line; pin. Topstitch through all layers.

Making ties: Press each bias strip in half lengthwise, wrong sides facing. Open crease of fold, and with wrong sides facing, bring cut edges to meet at the center fold; press. Refold along center and press, creating a double-fold bias binding.

Attaching ties to each skirt: Cut a diagonal slash from center opening of skirt to one outside corner (through all layers). Folding raw edges of tie under, slip one binding tie over each edge of slash. Pin, leaving excess length of ties at center hole; stitch in place.

POCKET STOCKING

You need: ¹/₂ yd white fabric for cuff and lining; 1 package of white piping; 1 yd of 3"W sheer white ribbon for cuff and pocket; 1 yd of ¹/₂"W white satin ribbon; ¹/₂ yd of ⁷/₈"W white satin ribbon; flower-shaped buttons; pearl teardrop-shaped bead; ¹/₂ yd crystal bead trim; small white tassel; sewing supplies.

Cutting fabric: Enlarge stocking and pocket patterns (this page); add ¹/₂" seam allowance to each before cutting out. Fold stocking fabric in half. Use pattern to cut four stockings (two for stocking, two for lining) from fabric. Cut a 15¹/₂" length of 3"W ribbon for cuff. Use pattern to cut two pockets from 3"W ribbon.

Making pocket: *When sewing, match right sides and raw edges and use a ¹/₂" seam, unless noted.* Leaving an opening for turning, sew pocket pieces together; turn. Slipstitch opening closed. Sew a 4" length of ¹/₂"W ribbon on pocket, folding ends to back of pocket. Sew pearl bead and one button to pocket. Sew pocket to stocking front, leaving top edge open. Slipstitch crystal bead trim along side and bottom edges of pocket.

Making stocking: Baste piping to side and bottom edges of stocking front. Sew stocking pieces together, leaving top edge open; turn. Baste piping around top edge of stocking. Fold a 7" length of ¹/₂"W ribbon in half for hanger. With raw edges even, pin ribbon ends to upper back edge on right side of stocking. Sew lining pieces together, leaving top edge open and leaving an opening for turning. Do not turn. Slip stocking in lining with right sides facing. Sew top edges together. Turn stocking through opening in lining. Slipstitch opening closed. Push lining down into stocking.

Adding cuff: Sew ¹/₂"W ribbon along one long edge (top) of cuff piece. Sew ⁷/₈"W ribbon ³/₄" from other long edge. Stitch short ends of cuff together, making a loop; turn. Slip cuff over stocking. Slipstitch in place along top edge.

Finishing: Sew buttons along bottom of cuff. Sew tassel to cuff.

Pocket Stocking
1 Square = 1"

Monochrome Monogram Stocking
1 Square = 1¹/₄"

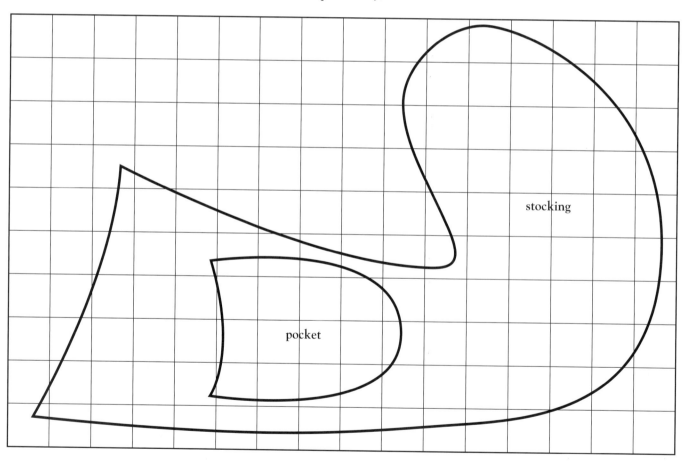

stocking

pocket

MONOCHROME MONOGRAM STOCKING

You need: 1 yd white linen for stocking and cuff; ²/₃ yd white cotton for lining; white rayon thread (for machine embroidery) or embroidery floss; 7" of white ribbon for hanger; 1¼ yds crystal bead trim; 1¼ yds pearl bead piping; sewing supplies.

Cutting fabric: Enlarge pattern (page 140); add ½" seam allowance before cutting out. From linen, cut one 19" x 8" cuff. Fold remainder of linen in half. Use pattern to cut two stockings from folded fabric. Repeat to cut two stocking linings from cotton.

Embroidering cuff: *You may use an embroidery sewing machine and its monogram settings/software, or you may hand embroider monogram using a calligraphy book as a guide.* On cuff, mark placement of center of monogram 5" from left (short) edge and 3" from top (long) edge. Embroider monogram.

Stitching stocking: *When sewing, match right sides and raw edges and use a ½" seam, unless noted.* Sew stocking pieces together, leaving top edge open; turn. Sew lining pieces together in same manner; do not turn. Slip lining in stocking with wrong sides facing. Fold ribbon in half, matching ends. With all raw edges even, pin ribbon ends to upper back edge of lining.

Adding cuff: Pin pearl bead piping to bottom edge of cuff on right side. With zipper foot, stitch close to piping. Press seam allowance to wrong side. Sew crystal bead trim 1" from bottom of cuff. Stitch short ends of cuff together, making a loop. Position cuff inside stocking with right side of cuff facing right side of lining. Stitch cuff to stocking. Fold cuff down over stocking.

Monogrammed Snowflake Stocking
1 Square = 1"

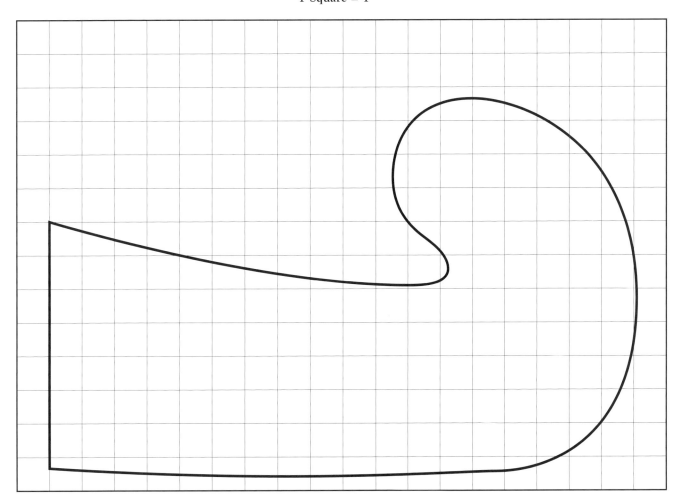

KNITTED WHITE STOCKING

You need: Wool yarn, 50 gram hanks – 2 hanks natural and 1 hank blue; double pointed needles (dpn), one set (4 needles), size 7 (4.5mm) OR SIZE NEEDED TO OBTAIN GAUGE; stitch marker; yarn needle; crochet hook, size G/6.

Knit Abbreviations: Listed on page 156.

Gauge: In St st (k on RS; p on WS), 22 sts and 31 rows = 5". TAKE THE TIME TO CHECK YOUR GAUGE.

Stocking: Beg at top edge on one needle and natural, cast on 48 sts. Divide sts on three needles. Join; take care not to twist sts on needles. Mark end of rnd and sl marker every rnd. Work in k1, p1 rib for 1 1/2". Change to St st; work until leg measures 13 3/4" from beg.

Heel: Sl 16 sts from first needle onto empty needle, then sl last 8 sts from third needle onto other end of the same needle – 24 heel sts. Divide rem 24 sts onto two needles to be worked later for instep. Cutting yarn and reattaching at beg of row, work back and forth in rows on heel sts only as follows: **Row 1 (WS)** – Sl 1 purlwise, purl to end. **Row 2 (RS)** – Sl 1 purlwise; knit to end. Rep these two rows until heel measures 2", end with a RS row.

Turn heel: **Next Row (WS)** – Sl 1, p12, p2tog, p1, turn. **Row 2** – Sl 1, k4, SKP, k1, turn. **Row 3** – Sl 1, p5, p2tog, p1, turn. **Row 4** – Sl 1, k6, SKP, k1 turn. Continue in this way, always having one more st before dec on every row until 16 sts rem.

Shape instep: **Next rnd (RS)** – With same needle pick up and k 8 sts along side of heel piece (Needle 1); with Needle 2, k next 24 sts (instep); with Needle 3, pick up and k 8 sts along other side of heel piece, then with same needle, k 8 sts from Needle 1. There are 16 sts on Needles 1 and 3; 24 sts on Needle 2 for a total of 56 sts. Mark center of heel for end of rnd. Continue as follows: **Rnd 1** – *Needle 1* k to last 3 sts, k2tog, k1; *Needle 2* knit; *Needle 3* k1, SKP, k to end. **Rnd 2** – Knit. Rep last 2 rnds 3 times more – 48 sts. Continue to work even until foot measures 8" from back of heel to beg of shape toe.

Shape toe: **Rnd 1** – *Needle 1* k to last 3 sts, k2tog, k1; *Needle 2* k1, SKP, k to last 3 sts, k2tog, k1; *Needle 3* k1, SKP, k to end. **Rnd 2** – Knit. Rep last 2 rnds 7 times more – 16 sts. Place 8 sts on two needles and weave to using Kitchener st.

Making hanging loop: With natural, cast on 4 sts, do not turn. * Sl sts to other end of needle and k4; rep from * until cord measures 5 1/2"L. Bind off. Join ends and sew inside stocking.

Snowflake: With tapestry needle and blue, work a 6-arm embroidered back-stitch snowflake, as shown in diagram (this page), on top of stocking.

Tie: With blue and crochet hook, work a single-crochet chain, 40"L. Weave through last rib row; tie bow.

LATTICE STOCKING

You need: 1 yd white fabric for stocking; 1/2 yd each of 3"W white satin ribbon, 2 1/2"W fancy ribbon and pom-pom trim for cuff; 2 yds gimp trim for lattice and hanger; 1 1/2 yds twisted satin piping; sewing supplies.

Cutting fabric: Enlarge pattern (page 143); add 1/2" seam allowance before cutting out. Fold stocking fabric in half. Use pattern to cut four stockings (two for stocking, two for lining) from fabric.

Creating lattice: Pin lengths of gimp trim on right side of front stocking piece, diagonally in crisscross fashion, spacing about 4" apart. Topstitch.

Making stocking: *When sewing, match right sides and raw edges and use a 1/2" seam, unless noted.* Baste piping to side and bottom edges on stocking front. Sew stocking pieces together, leaving top edge open; turn. Baste piping around top edge of stocking. Fold a 7" length of gimp trim in half for hanger. With raw edges even, pin hanger ends to upper back edge of lining. Sew lining pieces together, leaving top edge open and leaving an opening for turning. Do not turn. Slip stocking in lining, with right sides facing. Sew top edges together. Turn stocking through opening in lining. Slipstitch opening closed. Push lining down into stocking.

Adding cuff: Cut 13" lengths of 3"W ribbon, 2 1/2"W ribbon, and pom-pom trim for cuff. Arrange pom-pom trim and narrow ribbon on wide ribbon. Topstitch. Stitch short ends of cuff together, making a loop; turn. Slip cuff over stocking. Slipstitch in place along top edge.

Knitted White Stocking Snowflake

Lattice Stocking
1 Square = 1"

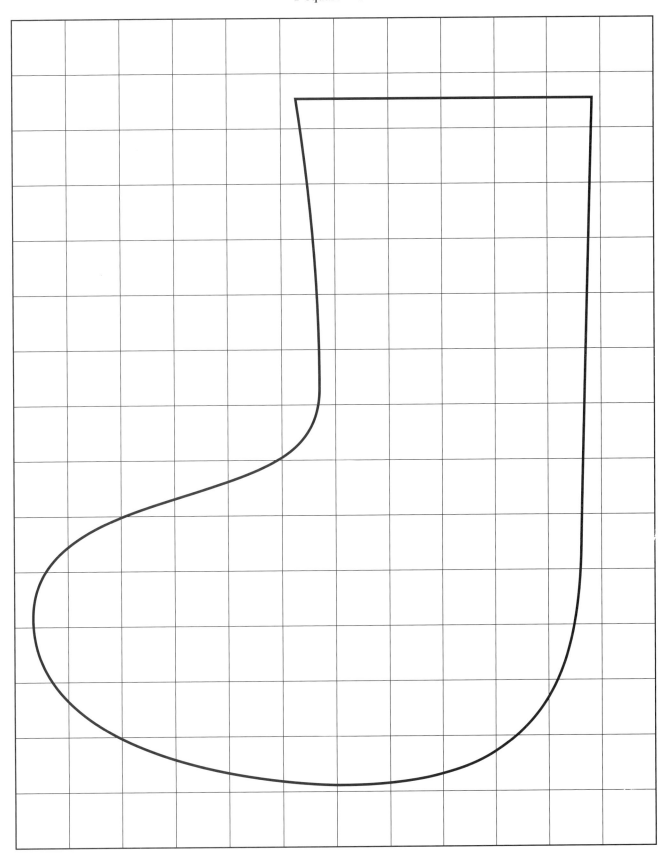

Fast & Festive:
accent on easy (pages 34-35)

EASY MANTEL TRIM
You need: White paper doilies; floral paper napkins; double-sided tape; beaded braid trim; straight pins; scissors.
To do: Arrange doilies, then napkins on mantel. Tape in place as needed to secure. Pin braid trim along edge of mantel.

FANCY FLOWERPOT
You need: Flowerpot or vase; two squares of contrasting fabric (size of squares equals twice the pot height plus width of pot opening); ribbon; sewing supplies.
To do: With right sides facing, sew squares of fabric together, leaving an opening for turning. Turn and press. Place flowers in pot. Place pot on center of fabric square. Gather fabric up around pot. Tie with ribbon to secure.

CURTAIN TIEBACKS
You need: Fresh or preserved magnolia leaves; artificial ivy; gold spray paint; glue gun; acrylic jewels; assorted ribbons; scissors.
To do: Spray paint leaves and ivy. Glue jewels to leaves. Tie curtain with several lengths of ribbon. Wrap ivy around curtain. Tuck in leaves.

NO-SEW TABLE RUNNERS
You need: Plain tablecloth; assorted widths of several different ribbons; small straight pins; scissors.
To do: Place tablecloth on table. Arrange ribbons across table in crisscross fashion to form runners. Pin ribbons in place in inconspicuous places.

SPARKLY CANDLES
You need: Hurricane-style candle holders; pillar candles; clear micro-beads; glass marbles.
To do: Set candles into holders. Pour beads and/or marbles into holder around candle.
Note: Do not let candles burn down close to beads and/or marbles.

red, white & true christmas
(pages 36-41)

PLAID HEEL AND TOE STOCKING
You need: Lightweight denim; raw silk plaid fabric; tassel trim; sewing supplies.
Making pattern: Enlarge stocking pattern (page 146) to 10$\frac{1}{2}$" tall. Make separate patterns to fit heel and toe of pattern. Add $\frac{1}{2}$" all around each for seam allowances. Cut out.
Cutting: *Denim* – Fold fabric in half. Cut stocking front and back following pattern. *Plaid* – Fold fabric in half. Cut two lining pieces following stocking pattern. Unfold fabric. Cut one toe and one heel piece following patterns. Cut one piece 3"H x width to fit stocking width where desired. Cut a 2" x 6" strip for hanging loop.
Embellishing stocking front and back: Press straight edge of toe piece $\frac{1}{2}$" to wrong side. Repeat for heel piece. Arrange toe and heel pieces on stocking front. Topstitch in place along pressed edges. Press long edges of 3"H strip $\frac{1}{2}$" to wrong side. Arrange on stocking front. Cut a piece of tassel trim to fit along bottom edge of strip. Place straight edge of trim under bottom edge of strip. Topstitch in place.
Sewing: *All stitching is done in $\frac{1}{2}$" seams, with right sides facing and raw edges even, unless noted.* Sew stocking front and back together, leaving top edge open. Clip curves; turn. Sew stocking lining pieces together, leaving top edge open and an opening along one side. Clip curves; do not turn. Place stocking inside lining. Sew top edges together. Turn through opening in lining. Slipstitch opening closed. Push lining down into stocking.
Finishing: Fold hanging loop strip in half lengthwise; sew long edges together. Turn. Fold strip in half to form loop. Stitch ends to upper back corner of stocking.

DIAMOND-MOTIF DENIM STOCKING
You need: Lightweight denim fabric; raw silk plaid fabric; star sequin appliqué; small star buttons; sewing supplies.
Making pattern: Enlarge stocking pattern (page 146) to 16$\frac{1}{2}$" tall; add $\frac{1}{2}$" all around for seam allowance. Cut out.
Cutting: *Denim* – Fold fabric in half. Cut stocking front and back following pattern. Cut stocking lining front and back following pattern. Cut a 2" x 6" strip for hanging loop. *Plaid* – Following photo (page 38) cut large diamond pieces for stocking front, adding $\frac{1}{2}$" for seams.
Embellishing stocking front: Press edges of diamond piece $\frac{1}{2}$" to wrong side. Following photo, arrange on stocking front, trimming as needed to fit. Topstitch in place.

Sewing: *All stitching is done in ¹/₂" seams, with right sides facing and raw edges even, unless noted.* Sew stocking front and back together, leaving top edge open. Clip curves; turn. Sew stocking lining pieces together, leaving top edge open and an opening along one side. Clip curves; do not turn. Place stocking inside lining. Sew top edges together. Turn through opening in lining. Slipstitch opening closed. Push lining down into stocking.

Finishing: Fold hanging loop strip in half lengthwise; sew long edges together. Turn. Fold strip in half to form loop. Stitch ends to upper back corner of stocking. Hand-stitch sequin appliqué to stocking. Sew buttons to stocking at corners of diamonds.

DENIM LACE-UP STOCKING

You need: Denim fabric; raw silk plaid fabric; velveteen fabric; large silver grommets; grommet setting tool; sewing supplies.

Making pattern: Enlarge stocking pattern (page 146) to 12¹/₂" tall. Extend front edge of pattern up into a point. Add ¹/₂" all around for seam allowance. Cut out.

Cutting: *Denim* – Fold fabric in half. Cut two stocking pieces for front and back. From stocking front, trim 1" from lower edge. Cut one 2"W x 6"H strip for hanging loop. *Plaid* – Fold fabric in half. Cut two stocking pieces for lining front and back. *Velveteen* – Cut a 1¹/₂"W piece to fit across lower edge of stocking front piece.

Sewing: *All stitching is done in ¹/₂" seams, with right sides facing and raw edges even, unless noted.* Sew velveteen piece to front piece. Sew denim stocking front and back pieces together, leaving front edge from upper part of foot to top opening unstitched. Clip curves; turn. Stitch lining pieces together in same manner; do not turn. Press raw edges along front of both stockings ¹/₂" to wrong side. Slip lining inside stocking. Topstitch stocking together along pressed edges only. Cut a 2"W piece of velveteen to fit around top of stocking, adding 1". Press edges ¹/₂" to wrong side. Fold strip over top edge of stocking and sew in place.

Adding "laces": Mark placement of grommets along both sides of open front edge. Following manufacturer's instructions, use grommet tool to set grommets where marked. Cut a 2" x 36" strip of velveteen for tie. Fold in half lengthwise and sew along long edge. Turn. Fold short ends ¹/₂" inside tube; sew closed. Lace tie through grommets.

Finishing: Fold hanging loop strip in half lengthwise; sew long edges together. Turn. Fold strip in half to form loop. Stitch ends to upper back corner of stocking.

PLAID TABLE TOPPER

You need: Large sheet of paper; plaid silk fabric; white grosgrain ribbon; wire-edged ribbon; sewing supplies.

Measuring: Draw tabletop dimensions on paper, adding ¹/₂" all around. Cut out. Measure around circumference of tabletop and multiply by 2 for skirt width. Cut one piece of fabric, obtained skirt width x 10" for skirt length (pieced as necessary). Use paper pattern to cut tabletop piece. Cut a piece of grosgrain ribbon the same length as lower edge of skirt.

Sewing: Press lower edge of skirt ¹/₂" to right side. Place ribbon on skirt even with pressed edge. Topstitch ribbon in place along long edges. With right sides facing, sew short ends of skirt together to make a loop. Sew two rows of basting stitches along top edge. Pull threads to gather skirt to fit around top piece. Sew gathered edge of skirt to top piece.

Finishing: Tie large bows from wire-edged ribbon and sew around edges of tablecloth.

BLUE AND WHITE UNDERCLOTHS

You need: Blue denim; white fabric; thumbtack; strong thread; sewing supplies.

Cutting (for each undercloth): Measure across tabletop plus 2 times distance from tabletop to floor; add 2" for hem. Cut a fabric square to the obtained measurement, piecing as necessary. Fold square into quarters. Thumbtack one end of tape measure to folded corner opposite loose edges. Stretch tape measure to ¹/₂ total obtained above. Draw an arc from fold to fold. Cut through all layers along marked curve. Open up.

Sewing: Press raw edge ¹/₂", then ¹/₂" again to wrong side. Topstitch in place to hem each cloth. For blue skirt, mark circle into quarters. With strong thread, sew running stitches where marked from floor to 8" from tabletop. Pull threads to gather and knot ends securely.

Plaid Heart Ornaments
Enlarge to desired size

Stocking Pattern
Enlarge to size indicated in instructions

Beaded Bird Ornaments
Enlarge to desired size

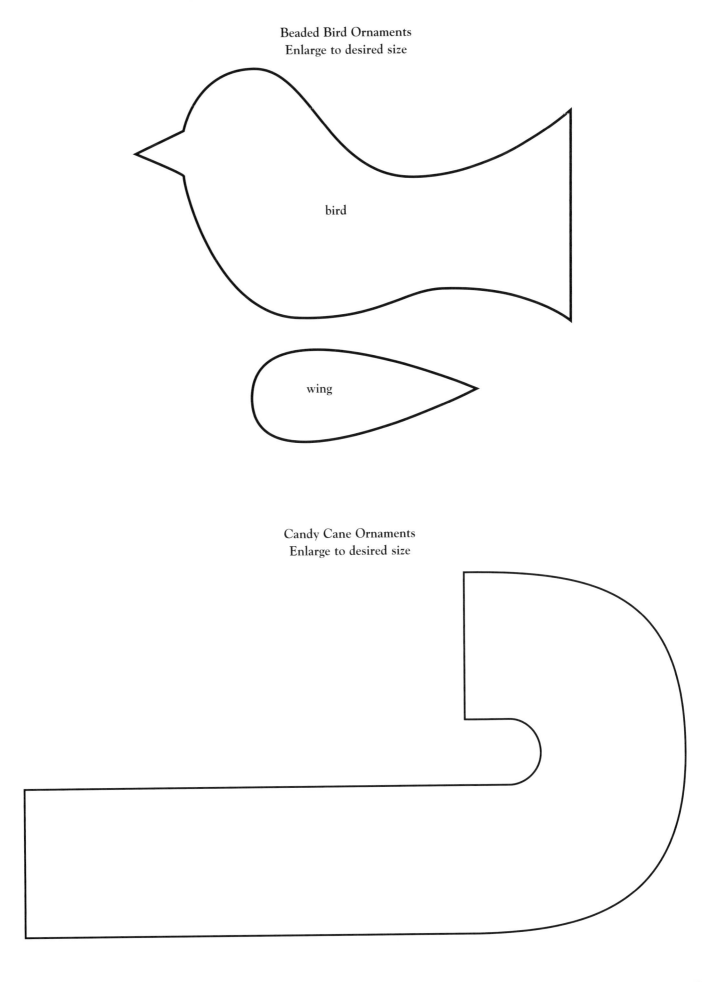

bird

wing

Candy Cane Ornaments
Enlarge to desired size

BALL ORNAMENTS

You need: 4"-dia plastic-foam balls; remnants of denim, plaid raw silk and velveteen; straight pins; string sequin trim; low-temp glue gun; scissors.

Cutting pieces: Trace full-size section pattern (this page); cut out. From remnants, use pattern to cut at least eight sections for each ball.

Covering each ball: Wrap each section piece around ball, holding in place with pins along the edges. Cover ball completely, overlapping pieces as desired.

Finishing each ball: Knot ends of a 6" length of gold thread together. Pin knot to center top of ball for hanging loop. Glue sequin trim over all edges of fabric pieces, covering pins.

STAR TREE TOPPER

You need: Remnants of denim, silk plaid, solid silk and velveteen; fiberfill stuffing; plastic mesh; string sequin trim; fabric glue; sewing supplies.

Cutting: Enlarge star point pattern (this page) as desired; add $1/2$" all around for seam allowance. Cut out. Using paper pattern, cut two points from each of five fabrics as desired.

Sewing: With right sides together and matching raw edges, sew five points together along short sides to make a star. Sew remaining five points together, positioning fabrics in same order as first star. Lining up fabrics, sew stars together, leaving a 2" opening between bottom points for turning. Clip corners; turn. Cut a 4" x $6^{1}/2$" piece of plastic mesh. Roll mesh lengthwise to make a 2"-dia circle and sew together to make a tube for inserting on tree. Stuff star firmly and slip mesh tube inside star. Sew opening of star around tube edge. Glue sequin trim over seams of star.

Star Tree Topper
Enlarge to desired size

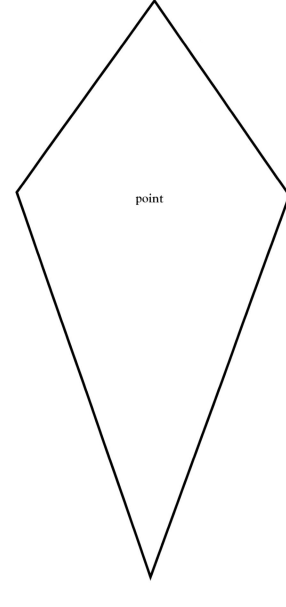

point

Ball Ornaments

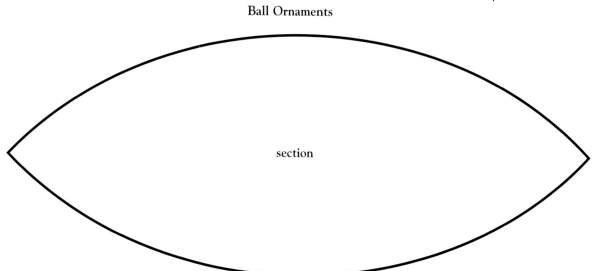

section

148

Fast & Festive:
frosty touches (pages 42-43)

STARRY WELCOME
You need: Rubber boots; floral foam for fresh flowers; distilled water; star-shaped ice-pop molds; lollipop sticks; fresh greenery; plastic wrap.

To do: Place lollipop sticks in ice-pop molds. Fill molds with water and freeze. Soak floral foam in water and wrap in plastic wrap. Place wrapped foam pieces in boots. Stick greenery and ice stars into foam.

ICY STARS
You need: Distilled water; 9" star cake pan; star stickers; fresh greenery; ribbon.

To do: Fill cake pan with water to a depth of ³/₄". If desired place fresh greenery in pan. Place ends of a length of ribbon in water to form hanger. Place cake pan flat in freezer. Freeze water. Unmold star. If desired, stick star stickers on ice mold.

STAR LAWN ORNAMENTS
You need: ¹/₂" thick exterior plywood; 1" x 2" wood studs; jigsaw; 1¹/₄" flathead wood screws; drill with bits; screwdriver; sandpaper; paint primer; white paint; polyurethane; paintbrushes; mini Christmas tree lights; glue gun.

Cutting: Enlarge star pattern (this page) to make three patterns – one 2' across, one 3' across, one 4' across. Cut desired number of stars from plywood. Leaving about 3" for border, cut out centers of stars. Cut lengths of studs — 27" for small, 29" for medium and 40" for large star. Taper one end of each stud into a point for inserting into ground. Line up stud with one side of star; screw in place, drilling pilot holes as needed.

Painting: Lightly sand stars and studs. Paint with primer. Paint with white paint. Paint with polyurethane. Position lights around edges of stars and glue in place. Stick studs in ground until stars stand firmly and securely.

Star Lawn Ornament
Enlarge to sizes indicated in instructions

merry mini trees
(pages 44-51)

Doghouse Topper
1 Square = 1"

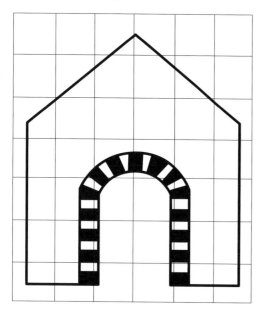

Paw Print Tree Skirt
Use pattern as is for small print; enlarge as
desired for large print.

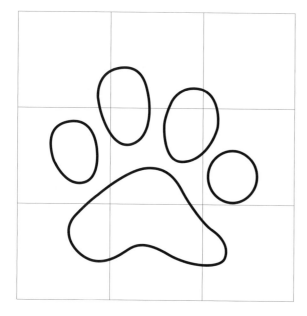

Fast & Festive:
fun for kids (pages 52-53)

PAPER CHRISTMAS WREATH
You need: 2 shades of green paper; assorted paper die-cuts in holiday themes; paper die-cut bow; jingle bells; glue gun; ribbon for hanger; cardboard; scissors.
To do: Trace hand shapes onto green paper; cut out. Draw desired size wreath on cardboard; cut out. Glue hands and die-cuts to cover wreath shape. Glue jingle bells to bow. Glue ends of ribbon to back of wreath to make hanger.

EDIBLE ORNAMENTS
You need: Green food coloring; coconut flakes; self-seal plastic bag; meringue powder; pretzel sticks; jelly candies; ice cream cones; small multicolored candies.
Preparing ingredients: Place coconut in bag; add small amount of food coloring and shake to coat evenly. Spread on a baking sheet to dry. Following instructions on meringue powder box, make royal icing.
Assembling: Push one pretzel stick into jelly candy to form tree trunk. Dip other sticks in icing; press onto trunk to form tree branches. Dip candies in icing; press onto branches for ornaments. To make evergreens, coat ice cream cone in icing; roll in dyed coconut. Let dry; shake off excess. Attach small candy ornaments same as for pretzel tree.

HOLIDAY GARLAND
You need: Craft foam sheets – red, white, green; craft glue; hole punch; red satin cord; small wood beads in assorted colors; $1/2$"W red grosgrain ribbon; scissors.
Making ornaments: Enlarge patterns (page 151); cut out. Trace onto foam; cut out. For each piece, cut contrasting underlayer of foam slightly larger. Layer and glue matching pieces; punch hole at center top.
Making garland: Knot one end of cord. String several beads onto it. Slip on ornament; pull cord back through previous bead or two to form dangle. Continue stringing beads and adding ornaments as desired until garland is desired length.
Finishing: Tie other end of cord close to last beads. Cut 9" of ribbon for each ornament; tie in bow just above ornament.

SANTA BELL

You need: 4" and 6" terra-cotta pots; paintbrushes; enamel paints – white, red, flesh; glue gun; 2 black buttons; 12" of 22-gauge wire; wire cutters; small metal bell; 1 yd of 1"W plaid ribbon.

Painting: Paint bottom and sides of both pots red and rims white; let dry. Referring to photo (page 53), paint half of side of large pot flesh for face; let dry. Mix red paint with small amount of white to make pink; paint cheeks. Paint red mouth on face; let dry. Paint tiny dot of white in center of mouth to highlight. Paint white hair and beard around face; let dry.

Finishing: Glue pots together at edges. Glue button eyes to face. Twist one end of wire through loop in bell. Slip other end of wire up through holes in pots so bell hangs inside large pot; twist other end of wire into loop. Slip ribbon through loop; tie ribbon in bow on top of small pot.

SNOWMAN TABLE TOPPER

You need: White pom-poms – two 2", two 1½", one 1", five ³⁄₄"; 5mm pom-poms – 3 black, 2 yellow, 2 red, 2 orange; craft glue; chenille stems – green, orange, black, 2 brown; 2 google eyes; black felt; craft foam – red, green, white; pinking shears; fine-point black marker; scissors.

Assembling snowman: Stack and glue five largest white pom-poms to form snowman. Glue black pom-poms to front of snowman for buttons. Cut ½" piece of orange stem for carrot nose; glue to face. Glue eyes above nose. Cut 1½" circle of black felt for hat brim. Roll black chenille stem into coil for crown. Glue crown to brim, forming hat; glue hat on head. Cut brown stem in half for arms. Cut 1" piece from each half for hand. Twist hand section around each arm, ½" from end; glue arms to body.

Assembling tree: Cut 4" piece of brown stem for trunk. Bend green stem into zigzag shape, getting wider at base; glue to trunk. Glue remaining 5mm pom-poms onto tree.

Assembling sign: Cut 4" piece of green stem for post. Cut 1" x 1½" pieces of red and white foam; trim white foam edges with pinking shears for sign. Glue white foam on red; write message. Glue sign on post.

Assembling table topper: Cut two white, one red and one green 5" square of foam; glue together for base. Glue snowman, tree, sign and remaining pom-poms to base.

Holiday Garland
1 Square = 1"

Artful Tote Chart

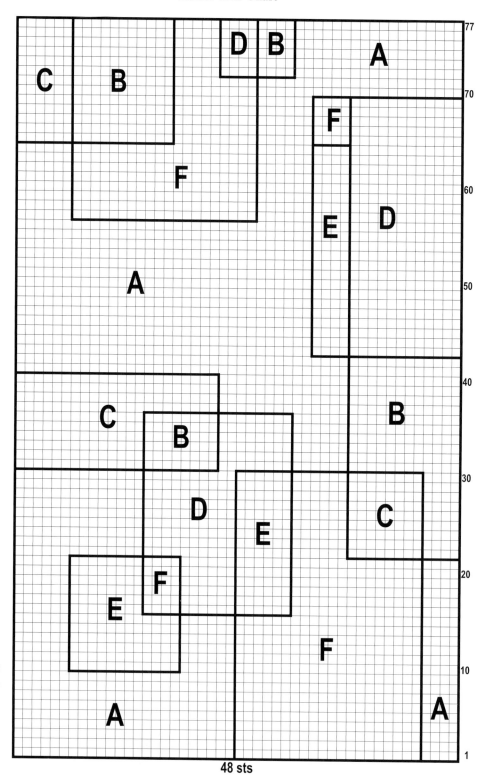

Color Key

Dark Green   (A)
Blue-Green   (B)
Blue   (C)
Dark Purple   (D)
Red-Brown   (E)
Light Brown   (F)

48 sts

ARTFUL TOTE

Size: 12"W x 14"H

You need: Mohair yarn, 1.5 oz/42g balls – 2 balls dark green (A), 1 ball each blue-green (B), blue (C), dark purple (D), red-brown (E), and light brown (F); size 8 (5mm) needles or size needed to obtain gauge; yarn needle; felt fabric; tortoise-shell handle; sewing supplies.

Knit abbreviations: Listed on page 156.

Gauge: 16 sts and 24 rows = 4" in St st. TAKE TIME TO CHECK GAUGE.

Tote Panel (make 2): With A, cast on 48 sts. Work in St st following chart (page 152). Read RS rows from right to left and WS rows from left to right. Be sure to twist yarns around each other on wrong side when changing colors to prevent holes. When all rows of chart have been worked, bind off with A.

Finishing: Cut two pieces of felt to same dimensions as tote pieces, adding 1/2" all around for seam allowance. Sew pieces together along side and bottom edges with 1/2" seam allowance for lining. With yarn needle and A, sew knit panels together at sides and bottom. Slip lining into tote bag and trimming away excess felt, sew together along top edge. Center handle along top edge and sew to tote with yarn needle and A.

DAD'S VEST

Sizes: Man's Small, Medium, Large and X-Large

Finished Measurements: Amounts given are for size Small; amounts for other sizes are in parentheses. Chest – 45 (48, 51, 54)"; Length – 24 (25, 26, 27)".

You need: Alpaca/wool/acrylic/polyamid blend yarn, 1 3/4 oz/50g balls – 12 (13, 15, 16) balls in blue; 1 pair each sizes 10 1/2 (6.5mm) and 11 (8mm) needles or sizes needed to obtain gauge; cable needle; stitch markers; 9" zipper; yarn needle.

Knit abbreviations: Listed on page 156.

Gauge: 10 sts and 14 rows = 4" in St st using larger needles. TAKE TIME TO CHECK GAUGE.

Cable pattern (over 36 sts): *Rows 1, 3 and 7 (RS)* – P1, k6, p1, k20, p1, k6, p1. *Rows 2, 4, 6 and 8 (WS)* – K1, p6, k1, p20, k1, p6, k1. *Row 5* – P1, sl 3 sts to cn and hold to back, k3, k3 from cn (6-st RC), p1, k20, p1, 6-st RC, p1. Repeat rows 1-8 for cable patt.

Making back: With smaller needles, cast on 56 (60, 64, 68) sts. Work in k1, p1 rib for 2 1/2", end with a WS row. Change to larger needles and work in St st until piece measures 14 1/2 (15, 15 1/2, 16)" from beg.

Shaping back armhole: *Next row (RS)* – Bind off 2 sts at beg of next 2 rows. Dec 1 st each side every other row twice – 48 (52, 56, 60) sts. Work even until armhole measures 9 1/2 (10, 10 1/2, 11)". Bind off all sts.

Making front: With smaller needles, cast on 56 (60, 64, 68) sts. Work in k1, p1 rib for 2 1/2", end with a WS row. Change to larger needles. *Inc row (RS)* – K13 (15, 17, 19) sts, pm, p1, inc 1 in next 3 sts, p1, k20, p1, inc 1 in next 3 sts, p1, pm (there are now 36 sts for cable patt between markers), k13 (15, 17, 19) sts – 62 (66, 70, 74) sts. Cont in patt as established, working

center 36 sts in cable patt (beg with row 2) and rem sts in St st until piece measures 14 1/2 (15, 15 1/2, 16)" from beg.

Shaping front armhole: Work armhole shaping same as for back – 54 (58, 62, 66) sts. Cont in patt until piece measures 16 1/2 (17 1/2, 18 1/2, 19 1/2)" from beg, end with a WS row.

Shaping placket: Work 27 (29, 31, 33) sts, join a 2nd ball of yarn and work to end. Work both sides at once, with separate balls of yarn until piece measures 22 (23, 24, 25)" from beg.

Shaping neck: Bind off from each neck edge 4 sts once, 3 sts, once, 2 sts once – 18 (20, 22, 24) sts each side of neck. Work until same length as back, end with a RS row. *Next row (WS)* – Work 11 (13, 15, 17) sts, [p2tog] 3 times, k1; for 2nd side: k1, [p2tog] 3 times, work 11 (13, 15, 17) sts. Bind off rem 15 (17, 19, 21) sts each side for shoulder.

Finishing: Block pieces. Sew shoulder seams.

Knitting collar: With RS facing and smaller needles, pick up and k 57 sts evenly around neck. *Next row (WS)* – P1, *k1, p1; rep from * to end. Cont in rib until collar measures 7". Bind off in rib. Fold in half to WS and sew in place. Sew in zipper along placket and collar opening.

Knitting armhole bands: With RS facing and smaller needles, pick up and k 61 (65, 69, 71) sts evenly around each armhole. Work in k1, p1 rib for 2 rows. Bind off in rib. Sew side and armhole band seams.

SON'S VEST

Sizes: Boy's 6, 8, 10 and 12

Finished Measurements: Amounts given are for size 6; amounts for other sizes are in parentheses. Chest – 33 1/2 (35, 38, 40)"; Length – 18 (19, 20, 21)".

You need: Alpaca/wool/acrylic/polyamid blend yarn, 1 3/4 oz/50g balls – 8 (8, 10, 11) balls in gray; 1 pair each sizes 10 1/2 (6.5mm) and 11 (8mm) needles or sizes needed to obtain gauge; cable needle; stitch markers; 7" zipper; yarn needle.

Knit abbreviations: Listed on page 156.

Gauge: 10 sts and 14 rows = 4" in St st using larger needles. TAKE TIME TO CHECK GAUGE.

Cable pattern (over 34 sts): *Rows 1, 3 and 7 (RS)* – P1, k6, p1, k18, p1, k6, p1. *Rows 2, 4, 6 and 8 (WS)* – K1, p6, k1, p18, k1, p6, k1. *Row 5* – P1, sl 3 sts to cn and hold to back, k3, k3 from cn (6-st RC), p1, k18, p1, 6-st RC, p1. Repeat rows 1-8 for cable patt.

Making back: With smaller needles, cast on 42 (44, 48, 50) sts. Work in k1, p1 rib for 2", end with a WS row. Change to larger needles and work in St st until piece measures 11 (11 1/2, 12, 12 1/2)" from beg.

Shaping back armhole: *Next row (RS)* – Bind off 2 sts at beg of next 2 rows. Dec 1 st each side every other row twice – 34 (36, 40, 42) sts. Work even until armhole measures 7 (7 1/2, 8, 8 1/2)". Bind off all sts.

Making front: With smaller needles, cast on 42 (44, 48, 50) sts. Work in k1, p1 rib for 2", end with a WS row. Change to larger needles. **Inc row (RS)** – K7 (8, 10, 11) sts, pm, p1, inc 1 in next 3 sts, p1, k18, p1, inc 1 in next 3 sts, p1, pm (there are now 34 sts for cable patt between markers), k7 (8, 10, 11) sts – 48 (50, 54, 56) sts. Cont in patt as established, working center 34 sts in cable patt (beg with row 2) and rem sts in St st until piece measures 11 (11½, 12, 12½)" from beg.

Shaping front armhole: Work armhole shaping same as for back – 40 (42, 46, 48) sts. Cont in patt until piece measures 12½ (13½, 14½, 15½)" from beg, end with a WS row.

Shaping placket: Work 20 (21, 23, 24) sts, join a 2nd ball of yarn and work to end. Work both sides at once, with separate balls of yarn until piece measures 16 (17, 18, 19)" from beg.

Shaping neck: Bind off from each neck edge 4 sts once, 3 sts, once, 1 st once – 12 (13, 15, 16) sts each side of neck. Work until same length as back, end with a RS row. **Next row (WS)** – Work 5 (6, 8, 9) sts, [p2tog] 3 times, k1; for 2nd side: k1, [p2tog] 3 times, work 5 (6, 8, 9) sts. Bind off rem 9 (10, 12, 13) sts each side for shoulder.

Finishing: Block pieces. Sew shoulder seams.

Knitting collar: With RS facing and smaller needles, pick up and k 39 sts evenly around neck. **Next row (WS)** – P1, *k1, p1; rep from * to end. Cont in rib until collar measures 7". Bind off in rib. Fold in half to WS and sew in place. Sew in zipper along placket and collar opening.

Knitting armhole bands: With RS facing and smaller needles, pick up and k 40 (42, 46, 48) sts evenly around each armhole. Work in k1, p1 rib for 2 rows. Bind off in rib. Sew side and armhole band seams.

TODDLER TAM

Size: 19" around

You need: 3-ply 100% cotton yarn, 100 gr skeins – 1 skein each blue (MC), ecru (CC); 1 pair each sizes 4 (3.5mm) and 5 (3.75mm) or sizes needed to obtain gauge; bobbins; yarn needle.

Knit abbreviations: Listed on page 156.

Gauge: 20 sts and 24 rows = 4" in St st using larger needles. TAKE TIME TO CHECK GAUGE.

Note: Do not carry yarn across back of work; twist yarns together when changing colors to prevent holes.

Sl st patt: Row 1 (RS) – With CC, (sl 1 with yarn in back, k1); repeat across row. **Row 2** – (Sl 1 with yarn in front, k1); repeat across row. **Rows 3 and 4** – Change to MC; repeat Rows 1 and 2. Repeat Rows 1-4 for patt.

Making hat: Beginning at lower edge, with smaller needles and MC, cast on 98 sts. Beginning with p row, work 3 rows rev St st (p RS rows, k WS rows), 3 rows St st (k RS rows, p WS rows). Change to larger needles. **Row 7 (checked pattern)** – K9 MC, (k8 CC, k8 MC) 5 times, k9 CC. **Rows 8-16** – Continue with same colors in St st. **Rows 17-26** – Reverse colors; continue in St st in same patt of alternating colors. **Rows 27-28** – Change to MC only; work 2 rows St st. **Rows 29-34** – Change to

smaller needles; work 4 rows rev St st, 2 rows St st. **Rows 35-38** – Change to larger needles; work in Sl st patt, starting and ending each row with 1 St st. **Rows 39-42** – K1, (SKP, 14 sts in Sl st patt) 6 times, k1 – 92 sts; work 3 rows in Sl st patt, keeping in patt at decs. **Rows 43-46** – K1, (SKP, 13 sts in Sl st patt) 6 times, k1 – 86 sts; work 3 rows in Sl st patt, keeping in patt at decs. **Rows 47-50** – K1, (SK2P, 11 sts in Sl st patt) 6 times, k1 – 74 sts. Work 3 rows in Sl st patt, keeping patt at decs. **Rows 51-54** – K1, (SK2P, 9 sts in Sl st patt) 6 times, k1 – 62 sts. Work 3 rows in Sl st patt, keeping patt at decs. **Rows 55-56** – K1, (SK2P, 7 sts in Sl st patt) 6 times, k1 – 50 sts. Work 1 row in Sl st patt, keeping patt at decs. **Rows 57-58** – K1, (SK2P, 5 sts in Sl st patt) 6 times, k1 – 38 sts. Work 1 row in Sl st patt, keeping in patt at decs. **Rows 59-60** – K1, (SK2P, 3 sts in Sl st patt) 6 times, k1 – 26 sts. Work 1 row in Sl st patt, keeping in patt at decs. **Row 61** – Change to CC. K1, (k2 tog, k2) 6 times, k1 – 20 sts. **Rem rows** – Work in St st (10 CC, 10 MC) until 12 rows are completed. Reverse colors twice. Bind off.

Finishing: Stitch back seam. Tie knot at top.

AMERICAN QUILT

You need: Cotton fabric – 7 yds white, 1¾ yds blue, ½ yd red; 68" x 78" cotton batting; embroidery hoop; 3 skeins red embroidery floss to match red fabric; book of redwork embroidery designs (or use any simple outline motifs for embroidery; you may choose to draw your own motifs); tracing paper; transfer paper; cutting mat; circle template; air-soluble fabric marker; sewing supplies.

Cutting: From white fabric, cut twenty 8" embroidery squares, seventeen 2" x 42" sashing strips; two 7" x 62½" side border strips, two 7" x 64" upper/lower border strips and one 70" x 80" backing, pieced as needed. From blue fabric, cut twenty-two 2" x 42" sashing strips. Cut remaining fabric into 2"W bias strips, piecing together to make binding strip. From red fabric, cut six 2" x 42" sashing strips.

Embroidering: *Embroidery diagrams are on page 156.* Trace redwork designs (adjust size, if needed, so motifs are about 6½" square); transfer a motif to center of each embroidery square. Using 2 strands of floss, embroider motifs using desired stitches, such as stem stitch, running stitch and French knots. Trim each embroidery square to 7½" square, centering motifs.

Making corner squares: *All stitching is done in ¼" seams, with right sides facing and raw edges even, unless noted. Press seams toward darker fabric after stitching each seam. Measure sewn strips occasionally to ensure straight lines.* Stitch a red sashing strip to each long edge of a white sashing strip. Make a total of 3 red/white/red striped pieces in same way. Stitch a white sashing strip to each long edge of a blue sashing strip. Make another white/blue/white striped piece in same way. Using rotary cutter, cut each strip into 2" lengths. Stitch a red/white/red piece to each long edge of a white/blue/white piece to make thirty 5" nine-patch blocks for corner squares.

Making sashing: Stitch a blue sashing strip to each long edge of a white strip. Make a total of 10 blue/white/blue striped pieces in same way. Using rotary cutter, cut forty-nine 7½" sashing pieces.

Assembling quilt top: Stitch 6 corner squares to 5 sashing pieces, alternating pieces, to form vertical sashing row. Make a total of 5 sashing rows in same way. Stitch 6 sashing strips to 5 embroidery squares, alternating pieces, to form vertical embroidery row. Make sure all embroidery squares are facing same direction. Make a total of 4 embroidery rows in same way. Stitch sashing rows to embroidery rows, matching seams and alternating rows to form quilt top. Make sure all embroidery squares are facing in same direction. Using circle template and fabric marker, mark a row of 5½"W scallops, 1" deep, ½" from one long edge of each border strip. Staystitch ¼" from each marked line on each border strip. Stitch side borders to quilt top, scalloped edges out. Stitch upper and lower borders to quilt top, scalloped edges out.

Quilting: Layer backing (face down), batting and quilt top (face up); baste layers together. Quilt as desired through all layers, stopping ¼" from staystitching. Trim front, batting and backing along scallop markings; baste close to edges.

Binding: Fold binding in half lengthwise, right sides out; press. Pin binding to right side of quilt, raw edges even; stitch in ¼" seam, overlapping ends. Press binding outward; fold to back of quilt. Slipstitch binding to back of quilt.

ALPHABET BOOKENDS

You need (for pair): Thick corrugated cardboard; craft knife; craft glue; cheesecloth; paintbrushes; bronze metallic paint; 32" of 1" x 4" pine; 8" x 16" piece of ¼" plywood; saw; wood glue; nails; hammer; yellowed document; decoupage medium; acrylic paints – gold, red, raw umber; gloss varnish; glue gun.

Making letters: Write or type letters "A" and "Z," then enlarge to 6½"L. Trace each letter twice on cardboard. Cut out using craft knife. Glue layers together, wrap with cheesecloth and glue ends to secure. Paint with a thick coat of bronze paint.

Cutting each bookend: From pine, cut one 8"L piece and one 6¾"L piece. From plywood, cut one 7½" x 8" piece (backing).

Assembling each bookend: Set 6¾" pine piece upright on one end of 8" pine piece, at right angles. Use wood glue, then hammer and nails, to glue/nail pieces together. Glue/nail plywood backing to edges of pine.

Decoupaging: Photocopy document in various enlargements. Tear in large and small pieces. Brush decoupage medium on backs; adhere to wood.

Painting: Thin paints with water to make a wash. Brush onto papered bookends, leaving some areas unpainted. When dry, apply varnish.

Finishing: Hot-glue letter inside bookend, as shown in photo (page 58).

STAMPED FRAME

You need: Unfinished wooden picture frame; paintbrushes; acrylic paints in 2 contrasting colors; rubber stamp in desired motif; mat board; craft knife; craft glue.

To do: Paint frame in lighter color; let dry. Brush remaining color of paint onto stamp; press onto frame as desired. Let dry. Cut mat board to fit frame opening. Cut center of mat board for photo opening. Glue mat board in frame opening.

Folksy Appliquéd Pillow
1 Square = 1"

basic how-to's

HOW TO ENLARGE PATTERNS

We recommend making enlargements on a copier – it's fast and accurate. Use the "enlarge" button; repeat copying and enlarging until you get the desired size. For some patterns, you may also use the grid method: Copy the pattern, one square at a time, onto 1" graph paper to get a full-size pattern.

SEWING SUPPLIES

Most sewing projects require the following basic supplies. Your project may not require every item.

Fabric marking pen or pencil
Ruler
Scissors
Sewing machine
Straight pins
Tape measure
Thread to match fabrics
Tracing paper (for making patterns)

KNIT ABBREVIATIONS

beg = begin, beginning
bet = between
CC = contrasting color
cn = cable needle
cont = continue
dec(s) = decrease(s)
g = grams
in(s) or " = inch(es)
inc = increase
incl = including
k = knit
lp(s) = loop(s)
MC = main color
p = purl
patt(s) = pattern(s)
pm = place marker
psso = pass slip stitch over
rem = remaining
rep = repeat
rev St st = reverse Stockinette stitch
rib = ribbing
RS = right side
rnd(s) = round(s)
skn(s) = skein(s)
sk = skip
SKP = sl 1, knit 1, pass slip stitch over knit stitch
SK2P = sl 1, k2 tog, pass slip stitch over knit stitch
sl = slip
sl st = slip stitch
sp(s) = space(s)
st(s) = stitch(es)
St st = Stockinette stitch
thru = through
tog = together
work even = work without inc or dec
WS = wrong side
yd(s) = yard(s)
yo = yarn over
* = repeat whatever follows the * as many times as specified
( ) and [ ] = do what is in the parentheses and/or brackets the number of times indicated.

EMBROIDERY

Running stitch

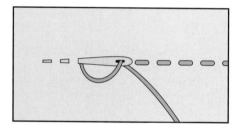

Cross Stitch

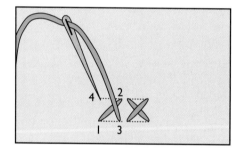

Back Stitch

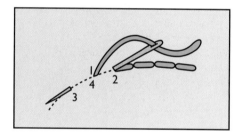

Blanket Stitch

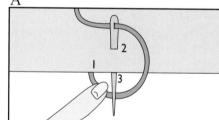

French Knot

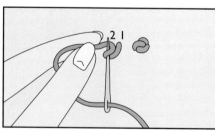

Stem Stitch

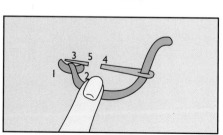

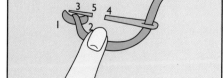

how-to's index

recipe index

credits

To the talented people who helped create the following projects and recipes in this book, we extend a special word of thanks:

- Samantha Bellucci: *Tiered-Ball Tree Topper*, pg. 31; *Plaid Table Topper*, pg. 39; *Star Tree Topper*, pg. 40; *Star Lawn Ornaments*, pg. 43.
- Amy Albert Bloom: *Gilded Reindeer*, pg. 17.
- JoAnn Brett: *Meringue Snowmen, Meringue Christmas Trees*, pg. 82; *Mocha Meringue Kisses, Basketweave Boxes*, pg. 84; *Cranberry-Orange Cream-Filled Meringue Torte*, pg. 86; *Meringue Poinsettias*, pg. 87.
- Brother International Corporation: *Monogrammed Snowflake Stocking, Monochrome Monogram Stocking*, pg. 32.
- Janis Bullis: *Chiffon Tree Skirt*, pg. 31; *Pocket Stocking, Lattice Stocking*, pg. 32.
- Mary Ellen Cocchi: *Wrapping Paper Pictures for Pet Tree*, pg. 47.
- Michele Crawford: *Boot Stocking, Green Velvet Stocking with Ruffled Cuff*, pg. 8.
- Abby Damrauer: *Goody-Filled Paper Cone*, pg. 26.
- Patsy David: *Santa Bell*, pg. 53.
- Teva Durham: *Chill-Chaser Scarf and Hat*, pg. 54.
- Bonnie Epstein: *Embroidered Star*, pg. 28; *Embroidered Dove*, pg. 31.
- Michele Filon: *Holiday Garland*, pg. 53.
- Stephanie Gildersleeve: *Toddler Tam*, pg. 55.
- S.F. Goldberg: *Button People*, pg. 56.
- Lori Hellander: *Harlequin Plates, Beaded Napkin Rings*, pg. 18.
- Leslie Hemmings: *Ribbon Sock, High-Heeled Silk Stocking, Jester Boot, Velvet Elf Bootie*, pg. 16.
- Susan M. Hinckley: *Tassel Ornaments*, pg. 9; *Advent Calendar Triptych, Advent Envelopes*, pg. 12; *King-Size Candlesticks*, pg. 15; *Doghouse Topper for Pet Tree*, pg. 47; *Wooden Place Mats*, pg. 59; *Folksy Appliquéd Pillow*, pg. 61.
- Diane Hogle: *Crushed-Velvet Bear*, pg. 24.
- Margot Hotchkiss: *Beribboned Footstool*, pg. 24.
- Samea Husein: *Beaded Ornaments for Golden Wire Tree*, pg. 46.
- Katherine Hyde: *Paper Dove Ornaments and Tree Topper*, pg. 7.
- Inga Johns and Chris Wallace: *Advent Calendar Chair*, pg. 13.
- Luba Kierkosz: *Denim Faux-Quilted Stocking, Plaid Heel and Toe Stocking, Diamond-Motif Denim Stocking, Denim Lace-Up Stocking*, pg. 38; *Alphabet Bookends*, pg. 58.
- Karen Laurence: *Starry White Tablecloth*, pg. 29.
- Amy Leonard: *Distressed Ribbon Frames*, pg. 57.
- Frederic Namur: *Curled-Paper Snowflakes, Jeweled Dragonflies*, pg. 24.
- Allison Pew: *Advent Goody Bags*, pg. 12.
- Rachel Tucker Richter: *Elegant Stemware Tassels*, pg. 26.
- Rebecca Rosen: *Knitted White Stocking*, pg. 32; *Dad's Vest, Son's Vest*, pg. 55.
- Roy Rudin: *Organza Mantel Scarf*, pg. 16; *Silk Tree Skirt*, pg. 17; *Silk and Velvet Place Mats*, pg. 18.
- Erin Shetterly: *Stamped Frame, Mosaic Frame*, pg. 59.
- Daphne Shirley and Sarah Shirley: *Beribboned Silk Stocking, High-Heeled Vinyl Boot, Slant-Cuff Satin Stocking, Feathered Shantung Sock*, pg. 20; *Christmas Tree Scarf*, pg. 22; *Shantung Napkins and Silk Table Skirt, Christmas Present Pouch*, pg. 23.
- Laurene Sinema, courtesy of Design Originals: *American Quilt*, pg. 57.
- Sue Ellen Stroum: *Harlequin Chair*, pg. 14.
- Karen Tack: *Jewel Candies, Bell and Star Cookies*, pg. 19.
- Robin Tarnoff: *Red Velvet Stocking, Green Velvet Beaded Stocking*, pg. 8; *Velvet Tree Skirt*, pg. 9; *Jester Doll*, pg. 14; *Beaded Bird Ornaments*, pg. 41.
- Cindy Tower: *Golden Pears, Letter Ornaments, Sheet-Music Ornaments*, pg. 7; *Pet Photo Frames, Paw Print Tree Skirt for Pet Tree*, pg. 47.
- Vogue/Mokuba: *Keepsake Frame*, pg. 61.
- Jim Williams: *Twelve-Point Star, Braided Star and Beaded Bell Ornaments, Velvet Cones and Balls*, pg. 17.
- Holly Witt, courtesy of Design Originals: *Snowman Table Topper*, pg. 53.
- And of course, special thanks to the expertise of the *Family Circle* Food Department.

Special acknowledgment is given to the following *Family Circle* photographers:

- Antonis Achilleos: pg. 22; top right, pg. 67; pg. 111.
- John Bessler: pgs. 6-11; top left, pg. 12; right, pg. 13; top left, bottom left, pg. 26; top, pg. 27; pgs. 34-41; top right, center right, pg. 53; bottom left, pg. 57; bottom, pg. 58; top left, pg. 59; pg. 60; top left, bottom left, pg. 61.
- Lydia Gould Bessler: left, pg. 13; bottom right, pg. 26; bottom, pg. 27.
- Monica Buck: top right, pg. 26; pgs. 44-47, 52; bottom left, pg. 55; bottom right, pg. 56; top left, pg. 57.
- Steve Cohen: pg. 62; bottom right, pg. 96; pgs. 68, 69.
- Katrina De Leon: pgs. 76, 78-81.
- Peter Freed: pgs. 48-51.
- Brian Hagiwara: pgs. 65, 66; bottom left, pg. 67; pgs. 74, 82-87, 94, 98-101, 110, 112, 113; top, pg. 114.
- Kevin Lein: pgs. 20, 21, 23-25; top right, pg. 61.
- Michael Luppino: bottom, pg. 12; pgs. 29, 30; top right, bottom left, pg. 31; pgs. 32, 33, 77, 88.
- Matthew McCabe: pgs. 42, 43.
- Josh McHugh: top right, pg. 58.
- Steven Mark Needham: top left, bottom right, pg. 53; pgs. 64, 70.
- Dean Powell: pgs. 72, 73, 75; top left, pg. 96; left, pg. 114.
- Steve Randazzo: cover; top right, pg. 12; pgs. 14-19.
- Alan Richardson: bottom right, pg. 57; pgs. 89, 90, 92, 97, 108, 115.
- Mark Thomas: pg. 93.
- Ross Whitaker: left, pg. 28; top left, pg. 31; pg. 54; top right, pg. 55; pgs. 102-107.

We also wish to thank the following *Family Circle* prop stylists:

- Betty Alfenito: pgs. 108, 110, 112, 113; top, pg. 114; pg. 115.
- Denise Canter: pgs. 82-87; top, pg. 99.
- Cathy Cook: top right, pg. 74; pg. 111.
- Valerie Fisher: pgs. 62, 68, 69.
- Julie Gong: bottom right, pg. 96.
- Lauren Hunter: pgs. 65, 66; bottom left, pg. 67.
- Kathy Imlay: pg. 28; bottom right, pg. 31; pg. 54; top right, pg. 55.
- Edward Kemper Design: pg. 97.
- Luba Kierkosz: pgs. 76, 78-81.
- Kim Kushner: left, pg. 13; bottom right, pg. 26; bottom, pg. 27.
- Francine Matalon-Degni: pg. 64.
- Christine McCabe: bottom left, pg. 74; pgs. 94, 100, 101.
- Nancy Micklin: pg. 93.
- Maria Santana: pg. 77.

Thanks also go to the following *Family Circle* food stylists:
- A.J. Battifarano: pgs. 93, 110, 112, 113; top, pg. 114.
- Roscoe Betsill: top left, pg. 96.
- JoAnn Brett: pgs. 104, 106, 107.
- Bob Chambers: pgs. 89, 90, 92.
- Anne Disrude: pg. 115.
- Susan Ehlich: pgs. 62, 68, 69; bottom right, pg. 96.
- Elaine Khosrova: bottom left, pg. 74.
- Julie Miltenberger: pgs. 82-87, 102-107.
- William Smith: pg. 97; top, pg. 99; pg. 108.
- Andrea Swenson: pg. 64.
- Karen Tack: pgs. 65, 66; bottom left, pg. 67; pg. 111.
- Fred Thompson: top right, pg. 74; pgs. 76-81, 94, 100, 101.

In addition, we'd like to thank the following hair and makeup stylists:
- Margret Avery for the Stephen Knoll Salon: pg. 54.
- Dean Miermeister: pgs. 103, 105, 107.
- Roseanne Renfrow: pgs. 103, 105, 107.